Influence Human Behavior:

Learn The Art of Negotiation and People Manipulation, discover the Psychology Behind Persuasion and mind control, use dark Psychology for Manipulation and Mind Control

J.R. Smith

Table of Contents

Introduction

Congratulations on buying *Influence Human Behavior,* and thank you for doing so!

The following chapters will discuss strategies to defend yourself against persuasion that may be aimed at you. With positive psychology, empathy, and skills of understanding, you will be able to protect yourself from those who wish to manipulate you. There are plenty of books on this subject on the market—thanks again for choosing this one! Every effort was made to ensure it is full of as much useful information as possible. Please enjoy!

Chapter 1: The Psychology of Persuasion

Psychology, simply put, is the study and science of behavior and the mind. As a formal study, psychology is only a couple hundred years old. However, philosophers and ancient theologians of yore were addressing the problems and topics of psychology in their own ways. The human species has had its methods of addressing psychological problems since the dawn of time. Psychology came around as a focused, science-based, and empirically-rooted study of human behavior, emotion, and cognition.

History of Psychology

Psychology is rooted in many different disciplines, including philosophy, science, and art. The philosophy connections come from the impulse to think about problems and examine our thinking processes. Psychology has a great weight on the moral issues of our time. Whenever a practice is rooted in moral implications as psychology, there must be philosophical considerations. When we do philosophical studying, it prepares us to think. It doesn't teach you *what* to think—but rather *how* to think. Being able to think and work out problems coherently is important for not only psychology but other fields as well. Psychology is closely aligned with science because one of the goals of the study of psychology is to explore and investigate the mind, behavior, and emotion. Employing the scientific method can often best do this exploration. The scientific method has provided a huge foundation for the advancement of psychology, and without science, there would not be the field of psychology, as we know it today.

It is, of course, a meta-oriented study—how can you study something when you must view it through the subjective lens of what you are studying? Psychology, in its most basic form, tries to develop an objective view and measurement of the mind's processes, patterns, and development. The only way we can engage with the subject, however, is by using our human, subjective minds, which, as we know by now, are very limited to our personal experience and perspective. Hence, we are put in a bit of a bind. Our task is to be objective and scientific in the study of the mind, but we are forced to use our minds to do the studying, and we can't trust our minds to be objective. It is this catch with which we proceed as we venture into the study of psychology.

The study of psychology can basically be broken down into two methods: the quantitative and the qualitative.

A quantitative study is a method that wants to have clear measurements of everything and only looks at things that are measurable. For example, a cup of water measured in a measuring cup—this is a quantitative measurement. We can see how much water is in the cup, we can measure it with pre-existing tools, and we know from our experience of using the tools that they are pretty accurate. Therefore, we can be pretty confident in the fact that the cup of water *is* a cup of water.

Quantitative measurements can be applied to psychology. This mostly comes from behaviorism, and this sect of psychology is centered on using measurements of mental and emotional phenomena. One way this might be done is by using a depression questionnaire or answering ratings about different aspects of your experience—i.e., "On a scale of one to ten, how anxious are you?"

A qualitative study in psychology is rooted in phenomenology. Phenomenology is the perspective of studying experience. Rather than trying to get quantifiable data out of a situation, the phenomenologist will ask for descriptions of what the experience was like for a person. The qualitative study looks at our subjective experience and embraces the subjective, rather than trying to draw out data to provide empirical results. Qualitative study often takes the form of essays, interviews, case studies, and other forms of research. An opinion piece is usually mostly qualitative.

Psychology is the study of the mind, but what does the mind entail? The mind is a concept that is still argued to this day. What are the limits of the mind? Is there a difference between the mind and the brain? What domains are controlled by the mind? Is there a soul? These are questions that are still debated, and they still affect the study of psychology. The mind is the genesis for our thoughts. It is also the "control room" for the body. The mind encompasses the brain, which is the physical "hardware" that carries out tasks for the mind. The mind is like computer software, but a thousand times more intelligent than we could imagine and a thousand times more creative than we could expect a computer to be. The mind is a somewhat nebulous concept. It comprises our thoughts and directs our emotions. Our thoughts and emotions are functions of the mind. Emotions have a strong physical component but are still processed through and directed by the mind. The human mind is the most wondrous concept that we can possibly think of. It is the highest level of evolution. It is the apex of intelligence, creativity, love, and thought. The study of psychology, then, is very important.

Psychology is an attempt to diagnose what is "normal" and what is "pathology." Pathology occurs when someone has developed in a way that is not functional or has symptoms that cause problems in their lives. Essentially, pathology is "sickness" of the mind. Pathology could be presented as negative thoughts, hallucinations, or many other symptoms. Psychology also helps us to know when pathology is found and how to treat it. If someone's pathology is that they are depressed, psychology says that we can put them through treatments to help them get better. There are a variety of therapies and medications that exist for the treatment of mental and emotional health problems.

Of course, we are now developing knowledge on why it's important not to over-diagnose and try not to judge behavior that does not cause harm. If you think about the history of society's beliefs and development, you can see how attitudes have changed over the centuries. It used to be believed immoral for women to wear anything but dresses. Once, we didn't understand electricity, let alone the Internet. Hence, we are a part of our cultural and temporal context, and that will affect our psychology. What was considered pathological behavior fifty or a hundred years ago is now known to be natural. The attitudes of what is expected of people in Western culture are fairly restrictive, even in our day and age. Psychologists in our contemporary age should understand that they need to be careful not just to slap a diagnosis on every difficult or weird behavior, and in general, they should try not to overgeneralize people with a diagnosis. The diagnosis is really not that important in order to understand people. Understanding people comes from using your intuition and being a loving person. The diagnosis is just some words that are needed to be labeled for reference for healthcare providers and the general public. There is no need to classify someone as a certain type of person because of his or her diagnosis.

Indeed, there may be many more people around you with a diagnosis of a mental health disorder or illness than you think. There are certain conditions—like schizophrenia, depression, anxiety, or other disorders—that can be very hard to detect in casual conversation with someone. Schizophrenia is one that we think of as being a very drastic disease—with everyone with this diagnosis being viewed as a crazy person, with hallucinations and all sorts of crazy talking voices. This is *not* the truth. There are certainly extreme cases of schizophrenia that cause people to have very bizarre behavior, but there are many, many people living with mild or moderate cases of schizoaffective or schizophrenia disorder who are very functional and live and work in the same space as we do.

Psychology is an essential and important study. We need to be able to look at the mind from an outside perspective and try to find out what is going on. This is not only for the treatment of pathology but also for the advancement of our human species and for the well-being of our communities.

Many ancient civilizations researched the topics of philosophy, but it was not named as such. Ancient philosophy tends to deal with matters of the mind, and Socrates' method of questioning to find the truth rings true today. The questioning method is one of the foundations of talk therapy. There were philosophers in ancient Africa, which discussed emotions, the habits of the mind, depression, and thought disorders.

There are many parallels with the traditions of ancient Greek philosophers, ancient African philosophy, and ancient Buddhist philosophy. Buddhism is based on the teachings of the Buddha, which emphasize the middle path and detachment from self. These teachings, when viewed through the lens of the history of psychology, were an early example of man's tendency to look in on himself. By creating a detachment to the self, the Buddhists were embracing a way of thinking that let them stand back and observe the mind. The practice of mindfulness, which stems from ancient Buddhist practices, is popular today as a method of self-regulation and bolstering mental health. There exists a text from ancient Buddhism entitled "The Yellow Emperor's

Classic of Internal Medicine," which discusses theories of personality based on the yin and yang balances, mental disorders, and wisdom and sensation.

The Enlightenment in Europe around the 16th century was a time when psychology, helped along by Gottfried Leibniz, advanced as an area of study. Christian Wolff published important books on the topic, and Immanuel Kant mentioned the subject as well.

You've probably heard of studies involving rats, designed to modify their behavior. These types of studies have been tried over and over again with different hypotheses and subjects. These methods of studies are labeled as experimental psychology. This begins in Germany in the 1830s, when Gustav Fechner started to take measures of the human perception of stimuli. Once these initial studies were started that looked at the human perception of what we are experiencing and recording the data, the practice of experimental psychology exploded, and psychologists all over the world started practicing with experiments that were designed in similar or different ways that started to establish the practice of experimental psychology.

Back in the 1800s, there was a psychology society called La Société de Psychologie Physiologique in France. This consisted of scientists, psychologists, and other thinkers, who would meet to share thinking and research about psychology. The American Psychological Association was founded just before the dawn of the 20th century.

Wilhelm Wundt used scientific research methods to look at human reaction times to stimuli. He published a book called "Principles of Physiological Psychology," which talked about the connections between the science of physiology and the study of thought at behavior. Wundt thought that the study of psychology was the study of consciousness. He thought that you could use science experiments to study internal processes.

Edward Titchener was a major figure in American psychology. He was a student of Wundt's and came up with the theory of structuralism. He thought that you could break down human consciousness into smaller patterns. He used the process of introspection to train people to break down their responses and thoughts into measurable things.

American psychology, at this point, was still somewhat crude—the study of eugenics was still a standard topic in psychology classes. During WWI and WWII, the U.S. military established itself as a leading funder of psychology research and application. Psychology became a way for the government to influence people. Psychologists had a big role in the management of the economy, too.

Around the early part of the 20th century, Sigmund Freud was developing his method of psychoanalysis. This totally changed the landscape of the treatment of mental disorders. Freud was largely responsible for the formalization of talk therapy. This also established the case study technique.

The most major development in psychology after psychoanalysis came in the '40s and '50s with the study of behaviorism. Behaviorism can be known as a system of psychology but also as a sort of philosophy. This was a big shift from the previous theories that were prominent in psychology. Before behaviorism, most psychologists studied the conscious and unconscious mind. Behaviorism changed things up, and behaviorists strove to make psychology a more scientific practice. They wanted only to look at observable behavior. Observable behavior could be a dog ringing a bell or a mouse hitting a button when he knows he will get a reward.

Rounding out the 20th century, around the '60s and '70s, came Third Force Psychology. This was centered on the thought of Carl Rogers. Carl Rogers is known as one of the founders of this school of thought. Rogers took some cues from psychoanalysis but focused more on the power of free will and self-determination. Maslow is also a big name in Third Force psychology; he created a hierarchy of needs that described the needs of people throughout development. The Third Force psychologists focused more on the phenomenological study. They were more interested in discussing the experience and understanding the subjectivity of the mind. They also believed in the concept of self-realization, the thought that in each of us, there is a" true" or "authentic" self, which we can work to achieve through personal development.

Contemporary Psychology

Psychology today has many stains of thought and philosophy. There is a big emphasis on CBT, cognitive behavioral therapy, which incorporates aspects of behaviorism but tempers it with cognitive theory. There is DBT, developed in the '70s for the treatment of borderline personality disorder by Marcia Linehan. DBT is one of the more modern treatment approaches. It emphasizes coping, mindfulness, and skill learning.

This is where we are with psychology today: we have a couple of centuries of history. It's not much; especially if you consider how long some other formal studies have been around, like mathematics and art. However, we've come a long way in the past couple hundred years, and there is still more to go. The psychology field today is rich and diverse, with lots of different options and strains of thought. Some of them go together nicely, and some of them disagree. Psychology now has become a reflexive study, one that considers a sense of self-awareness about its past and context.

Psychology and those who study it should be totally considerate of the cultural context of its ideas and patients. People don't exist in a vacuum. People are very complicated, and they are deeply affected by where they grew up. People who grow up in rural areas might have different traditions that those who grew up in urban areas. People of different races have different cultural values and different traditions. Throughout psychology, women have not been sufficiently represented, in research or in prominent roles. Psychology research has been unfairly centered toward maleness. These are all considerations that have to be taken into account when forming a new theory on psychology. For someone with a particular cultural value, they might think of body language in the form of contact, like hugging, to be invasive. Another person, however, could've grown up with a very touchy family who likes to hug. They both are fine, and either way is a find way to grow up, and one shouldn't be a preference over the other. This is just one example of a cultural difference that could lead to a divide.

These kids of multicultural considerations and postmodern topics are at the forefront of psychology right now. Psychologists are now realizing the depth and meaning of family of origin and cultural context, and are starting to learn how to employ methods to be inclusive to all sorts of people from different ethnicities, religions, and backgrounds.

Out of all of the characters that exist in the history of psychology, Sigmund Freud might be the most influential of them all. His "talking cure," talk therapy, revolutionized the treatment of mental disorder and started the field on a path of treatment that is still essential to this day. Freud developed his theory of psychoanalysis after years of working in medical settings. He was influenced by many factors, including mysticism and philosophy.

Sigmund Freud was born in Moravia, in the Austrian Empire. This is the area that would later be labeled as the Czech

Republic. His father was a wool merchant, and Sigmund had two brothers. The family was Jewish, and the children were raised in that tradition. Eventually, the Freud family found themselves struggling, and they left Freiberg, where they had been living, to move to Manchester, England.

Sigmund Freud went to the University of Vienna when he was seventeen. He joined the medical department, and worked with brains and zoological subjects, and helped to discover the neuron in the brain. When he became an MD, he started working at Vienna General Hospital. He did research on the brain and was a published and accomplished writer. He kept working in various areas of medicine, spending time in psychiatric clinics and asylum. He was appointed the prestigious position of lecturer at the University of Vienna.

Freud eventually resigned at the hospital and started a private practice. He described his work as specializing in nervous disorders. One of Freud's colleagues, Brentano, had introduced him to the concept of the unconscious mind. Along with this, he had done other research into the philosophy of the unconscious. There are many analogies between Freud's work and Nietzsche, but Freud claims not to have had Nietzsche as an influence.

His most important work, arguably, is the development of psychoanalysis. Freud went to Paris to study with a renewed neurologist. This visit was a catalyst for him to turn toward the practice of psychology and away from his neurological research. Freud started experimenting with hypnosis. The results of his hypnosis work were inconsistent. He started coming up with ways to get patients to free-associate. Free association is when you say whatever comes to mind, with no filter. Freud thought that instead of making suggestions to people through hypnosis, he could let them talk freely, and he could analyze the structure of their unconscious material. He thought that repression was the root of pathology. Psychoanalysis was the term that he started to use to describe his new method. In psychoanalysis, Freud believed that he could retrieve subconscious information that can help people understand why the way they are, in order to change it.

Alfred Adler was a psychologist who was working around the same time as Freud, but just a little later. He is classified as a psychotherapist. Psychotherapy is "talk therapy." It is often known as counseling. Adler took many ideas from Freud and was inspired by his work. Adler met with Freud in 1907 and became the president of the Vienna Psychoanalytic Society. Freud thought of Adler as a student and disciple of Freud's, but Adler didn't see it that way. He made his ideas separate from Freud's. Adler had a different way of interacting with patients; whereas Freud would have the patient la down and free-associate, Adler started to be more relationship-centric. He was a pioneer in the field of talk therapy.

Famous Psychologists

Jean Piaget was a psychologist from Switzerland, who did a lot of groundbreaking work in the area of childhood development. Piaget was educated in the psychoanalytic stain of psychology. He went to a school that was led by Binet, who had created the IQ intelligence test. Piaget helped to design and administer the IQ test. He noticed upon giving the test to children that children made certain types of mistakes that adults did not. This served as part of the foundation for his work. Piaget is most known for his stages of childhood development. The theories mostly have to do with cognitive and sensory perception. Piaget's stages are very interesting to learn about and can clue you into meeting children where they are and understanding how they experience the world.

B.F. Skinner was a psychologist and one of the most important figures in the study of behaviorism. He was a professor at Harvard and developed some very important concepts in the field of psychology. One of these concepts is operant conditioning. This is a method of learning that is based on punishments and rewards. There can be negative punishments and positive punishments; in this context, positive and negative have different meanings than usual. Negative in this context means taking something away. This could be a punishment or a reward. For example, positive punishment is adding something to the subject that is unpleasant, like spraying a cat with a spray bottle of water. Negative punishment would be taking away something that is pleasurable, for example, taking away a child's toy when they have been misbehaving. Skinner solidified the concepts of operant and classical conditioning. This had a huge impact on how psychologists were able to frame their research. This gave psychologists the philosophical support they needed to claim that their experiments were worth doing, and it helped them to prove that they were making progress. Behaviorism is all about measurability and objectiveness.

Similar to Piaget, Erik Erikson is best known for his work in the research of the development of humans. Erikson's theory, however, includes the entire lifespan, whereas Piaget's mostly looks at childhood development. Erikson's stages start at infancy and break down the lifespan from there.

The stages of Erikson are fascinating, and can also tell you a lot about where you are in your life. Until eighteen months, according to Erikson, we are in the Trust vs. Mistrust stage. This is where an infant learns to trust the world and their caregiver. This is an essential stage, where a person learns that the world is not only dangerous but also contains multitudes of love. From eighteen months to three years is the stage of Autonomy Vs. Shame and Doubt. In this stage, the infant must accept that they are not one with the mother anymore, and they have a separate body and consciousness that they are living in. Three to five years is the Initiative vs. Guilt stage. This is where the child is learning to interact and transport themselves, and at this stage, they must navigate the challenges of both initiative and guilt and incorporate an understanding and tolerance for each. The next stage is five to thirteen years old, and it is the struggle of Industry vs. Inferiority. At this stage, children are learning to do things and to be good at them. They might be playing sports or participating in the competition of relationships that high school often is. They may have pressure from their parents to do well in school. The next stage is Identity vs. Role Confusion. In this stage, young people start to develop their identity in the world, and they must integrate a sense of identity to avoid the feeling of confusion, which happens when a person is not fully integrated with the experiences they have had in the past and their current emotional and mental life. The next stage is Intimacy Vs. Isolation. This stage is where a person has hopefully developed an identity, which they can have with a sufficient amount of detachment. What comes after this is the ability to be deeply intimate with people. This could be a marriage, or it could be reflected in friendships or other relationships. The ages from forty to sixty-five reflect the struggle of Generativity vs. Stagnation. This is a stage where a person has developed an identity and a sense of self-security and starts to have the need to "generate" life or creative projects into the world. The great struggle in this phase is to feel like one's life is productive. After sixty-five, Erikson suggests that the final phase of life is Ego Integrity Vs. Despair. People at this age either will be able to cope with the realization that death is upcoming, or they will find themselves despairing.

Understanding Bias

Bias is a natural human trait. Humans have the need to make classifications around things. We classify different individuals, different foods, clothes, ways of living, etc. We put things in boxes so that we can store the boxes with other similar things so that we can have our consciousness organized. It is not something that you should blame anyone for. It is a natural thing that our minds do without thinking. Your context will have a lot of effect on your bias. If you are from Norway, you will think that Norwegian things are normal. You will have experienced the winters that exist in Norway, and eaten the traditional food of Norwegian culture. This is your cultural context. You may have religious traditions as part of your cultural context. You may have ideas about sex, art, or many other things. This cultural context is how you experience the world. The family has a big part in this, too.

We grow up in a certain context, and we learn to categorize and organza the world around us according to this context. This gives us biases. It is not unnatural to develop biases out of this; it is just a thing that happens. Fortunately, humans are capable of a great deal of development, change, and growth in the lifespan, and we can learn to analyze our biases. When we analyze our biases, we can see what has the truth, what is unfair, and which biases to keep and which to throw away.

Let's say Tina is from a small town in the Midwest. She was born in Middletown, Nebraska, and her family moved to

Springfield when she was seven. In Springfield, she experienced a wider range of cultural context than she did before the age of seven, but her cultural context is still centered around the Midwest U.S. she grows accustomed to eating beef and chicken, which is common in that part of the world and learns to expect certain things in her meals. When Tina becomes college-aged, she travels to Kansas City to pursue a degree in agricultural studies. She decides to live in a dorm and is assigned to a random roommate who is also studying agricultural studies. The two get along quite well; her roommate, Jen, is from Hawaii and has been experiencing the continental U.S. for the first time. Jen's parents are vegetarians; it is part of their faith tradition, and it is how they prepare all of their meals. Jen, of course, became a vegetarian too. Her parents did not force this on her, and they actually provided her with education about other faith traditions and taught her to be open-minded. However, Jen likes to reduce her effect on the environment by avoiding consuming meat. At first, this seems absurd to Tina; no one was a vegetarian where she grew up. People were expected to eat and enjoy meat. It provided important protein that was sometimes hard to find. Jen has grown up with a different set of circumstances, which led her to a different lifestyle. After a while, Tina starts to become understanding of Jen's choices and joins her in vegetarian meals once in a while. The lifestyle choice of vegetarianism has now become normalized to Tina, and she gets it. Before, she had a bias towards vegetarianism. She felt that it was silly, unnecessary, and something she could never understand. She now understands it by befriending a person who has a different lifestyle choice than she.

If we look at psychology, we can find a lot of explanations for bias. Sometimes, people have associations with things from a very young age. If you had some linguine alfredo when you were seven, and the food made you sick, you may not eat that particular dish again for 10 years. This is not a conscious bias that you have, but one that is based on an extremely physical experience that you had. It is not that you don't like those flavors inherently, but you have now associated the feeling of getting sick with the flavors that you had been experiencing. This can be seen in other situations, too. If you had a bad experience at a high school dance, where you were mocked for your appearance, you might find it scary to start dancing again. This has become your bias: dancing is dangerous and scary because people will make fun of me for it. Here's another example: Brian is what some would say resembles an artistic genius. He is a great songwriter and musician and is a great performer around town. He plays in multiple bands and is relatively successful as a creative. He doesn't like to be organized, however. It doesn't work for him. Whenever he tried to get organized as a young person, he always failed. He would buy calendars, and they would stay in one month for the whole year. He would try to keep track of assignments in an assignment book, but stop updating it after a few weeks. This is okay! Brian is a unique guy, and he functions well with his career and duties. However, this is his bias: he doesn't think much of being organized. Other people desperately need organization, and they rely on it for a sense of safety and stability. This is okay too! Brian will need to recognize his bias when working with others and compromise every once in a while, to make progress.

Understanding your own bias is crucial to developing critical thinking skills and problem-solving skills. Each of us has the potential to understand ourselves better people are able to achieve different levels of awareness and wisdom, and throughout life, you will discover your biases and be able to handle them effectively, if you do the work.

Doing the work looks different for everybody; for some, it may involve writing in a journal. Some people keep journals, noting the significant or insignificant events of their day, jotting down moods, attitudes, and things that are happening, and figuring their life out. This is a great way to examine oneself and see the patterns and biases that exist. You can take a look at previous journals and see how far you've come. Another way is to get a life coach or counselor. A third party can help you interpret your thoughts and become more effective in your critical thinking. Sometimes, you need someone to call you out on unhealthy thinking or point out problems in your story. This is not to make you out to be the villain, but rather that you can have a better sense of yourself and achieve more happiness for yourself and others.

Sometimes, our bias may be towards or against a certain personality type. Perfectionists are people who strive to be "good" and perfect. They want everything to be lined up in a row, organized and neat. They like to have everyone around them on board for the group project and are usually pretty charismatic. Perfectionists may be biased towards other people who are like them. If there is a person that they run into who is a romantic, for example, and this person doesn't care for structure, rules, or organization, this person might not get a fair shake from the perfectionist that they deserve. One should make sure to be accepting of the personalities of others and to not diagnoses their uniqueness as pathology. The romantic, in turn, can have a bias. They might consider the ideas of a person less if they don't feel that it fits into their view of the world Romantics tend to be dreamy, stuck in the clouds, focused on the meaningfulness, rather than productivity, and very creative. So, if a perfectionist comes along and tries to clean everything up and make everything good, the two might clash.

In order to do higher-level critical thinking, you must first know yourself. There are some ways that you can organize your thinking in this area. One is the method of VITAL Signs. VITALS stands for values, interests, temperament, around-the-clock, life mission, and strengths.

Let's talk about how you can use VITALS as a way to analyze yourself in some different categories. The first category is your values. You should look at your motivations in life to see where your values have lain in your past decisions. Maybe you have valued your physical health, and dedicated a lot of time to keep yourself in tips top shape. This is a great value to have. Another may be family. Have you kept yourself in a close relationship with your family, and maintained a good system with them? You may find that you have valued certain things too much. Maybe you have spent too much time chasing money or romantic love. This area is very tied-in with motivation. If you want to stay motivated and keep yourself in a trajectory, notice your vales and try to emphasize them in your work and life.

The next category is your interests. This is related to values, but slightly different. Interests are the kinds of things that you like to pursue. This could include hobbies, concerns, or passions. Some people find that they could never live the life of a working artist, but that a hobby of painting helps them to be emotionally secure, healthy, and in-touch with their emotions. Some people are able to make a living in their interests. It could be a wide range of things. Your interests could include political goals or activism or could involve relationships.

The next category is temperament. This describes how you are and your inborn preferences. Are you more of an introvert or more of an extrovert? What are the situations in which you feel most comfortable? This might take some analyzing or your social relationship and what they consist of. Some people like to do things out of the blue; driving by a restaurant they have never visited before; they will decide on a whim to try it out. Some people will never do this kind of thing and will drive past the restaurant every time unless you schedule a time to visit the restaurant beforehand.

A stands for around-the-clock. This refers to your biorhythms. Biorhythm is a term that describes the physiological or biological functions that we need to partake, and the time-based rhythms that they are bound to. Sleeping is a good example of something that contains biorhythm; it is something that starts around the same time every night (if you're lucky) and should end around the same time every day. Our biorhythms are an intimate way in which we are connected to the world. Our bodies are influenced by the rotation of the earth, and we are ultimately bound to its universal rhythm. Around-the-clock accounts for your sexual habits, your diet, your exercise, and all other biological functions. Examining these functions in our lives can lead us to a sense of clarity about how we organize ourselves.

Knowing yourself can seem like a simple task at first. It may be more complicated than you think. When you examine yourself and your choices, try to find the areas that are your weak spots. You also want to acknowledge your strengths. In fact, in examining your life, you may find that you are either a person who pays too much attention to their strengths or a person who pays too much attention to their weakness. If you are a person who pays too much attention to your strengths, you might find that you have a lesser ability to observe where you are weak or less capable than other people. People who have this tendency tend to be more on the narcissistic side. They tend to need to learn to be a little less selfish. This type of person likes himself or herself, which is good, but there are not able to give them reasonable feedback about where they need to improve in their lives. The other type of person is not able to witness his or her own strengths. They focus too much on their weaknesses and tell themselves that they are not worthy or good enough to be praised. They need to be a little more selfish. These two types of people represent a way to look at selfishness. The suffix "ish" has a meaning: belonging to, or after the manner of. Self*ish* means that you belong to yourself, you are focused on yourself, and you control yourself. This is a word that is often used with negative connotations, but I'd like to invite you to think of the word as a neutral value. Selfish merely means being about oneself. Some people need to be less selfish, for sure, but there are also a great many people who will need to learn to be more selfish. These are the people who were told that they didn't deserve anything. These are the people who don't know how to be appropriately self-interested and usually let others walk over them. When you are learning to know yourself, keep this in mind, and inspect your life for signs of having an imbalance in selfishness, in either direction.

Find Out What People Really Want

Many of us go through life, not knowing ourselves that this could be for many different reasons. Some were not taught at a sufficiently early age to self-examine. Some people repress this ability out of self-protection. Knowing yourself takes time and wisdom. Wisdom is not easily achieved. Take some time to try to think of how you're perceived in the world, not according to your perspective but to other peoples'. An interesting way to do this is the their-person method. The third-person method is where you imagine yourself as a character in a book, or a person who is observable to you that is not you. Instead of saying, "I went to work today and did a good job," say, "Tony went to work today and did a good job." You can do this to write your story so that you can have a sense of what is going on in your life. It could go something like this: Tina grew up in Wisconsin. Her parents loved her and did their best to raise her well. She didn't get enough attention on the skills of self-awareness, however, and not she is learning. Tina is doing a good job of hanging in there and keeping herself honest. In this example, Tina is kind to herself. Imagine if Tina had said something like this: "Tina grew up in Wisconsin. Her parents were okay, and they didn't give her enough attention. Tina is stupid because she is just now figuring out how to be self-aware." Now, this is not only untrue (Tina is not stupid, but it is unfair). This example is an exaggeration, and your negative self-talk may not be as bad as this—but when you write out your story in the third person method, you may notice some negative self-talk. That's okay, and that is part of knowing yourself. Knowing yourself sometimes can be easier if you think of yourself as the child version of yourself. You can be forgiving and gentle with this person because they are young and don't know yet how everything works in the world. Try to give a little bit of this to yourself. This will let you transition to your new way of living with greater rapidity and less stress. Change can be very hard. By being nice to yourself throughout the process, you can make the change easier. Remember, there are no techniques to make you perfect. Life is always probably going to be a little bit difficult. However, if you try to get through these changes with a good heart and kindness toward yourself, you can ease the challenges that lay ahead.

Chapter 2: Positive Psychology

Positive Psychology is a movement that started in the 1960s and 1970s in the US. Positive Psychology, or PP, started as a movement that applied the principles of psychology to everyday life so that laypeople who weren't necessarily educated in the depths of psychological theory could understand the concepts and try to apply them to their lives. PP is focused on letting people flourish in their lives, rather than trying just to allow them to live and survive. Do you see the difference? When we are just living and surviving, there is a mechanism that will help us to live longer, and the instinct to live is always there—but to truly flourish, humans have certain needs that must be met.

The Power of Smile

This makes up the difference between living and flourishing. When you are just living or surviving, your life may look a certain way. You may be meeting your basic needs as a person, i.e., a place to sleep, food to eat, a job, and other necessary aspects for human life. However, when you are flourishing, you will experience a deeper level of life on this planet. A person who is flourishing has deep experiences. They are able to integrate deep experiences of pain with deep experiences of joy and happiness. A person who is flourishing will be able to create connections with the people they want to. They will be close to their actual potential as a human being. They will also be able to help others gain what they need to become the self-actualized version of themselves. This flourishing comes from a few places. These include self-expression, connection, relationships, and meaning. Meaningfulness is a big one.

People strive for their entire lives to find meaning. Meaningfulness is something that we are not necessarily born able to find and see. It is something that we often have to work for. People are born in certain conditions; some people are born into poverty, and some are born into the middle class, and others are born into the higher echelons of society. Those people at the top may have an easier time, but they will all have to find meaning.

Meaning can come from the smallest things or the grandest parts of our lives; meaning is something that we must define for ourselves. Positive psychology looks for us to find meaning in our lives so that we can flourish.

Self-expression is another big part of flourishing. When people never express themselves, they will find that they are missing an essential part of human functioning. People must learn to express themselves without judgment in order to do this correctly. A connection is another aspect of flourishing that we require as humans. To flourish, most people must learn to connect with others. We are all born from another human, and this is the basic level at which we are required to relate to others. Humans must grow up at the hands of other humans, or else we will die. There is such a deep requirement for connection at this level. We must, at an early age, learn to connect with our family, or at least learn what family means to us, in order to find our place in the world. Without connection, human life is not human life.

Positive Psychology gives us a framework with which to pursue these life goals. PP is a way to learn how to get these things that we so desperately need. One of the ways to achieve these things is through positive thinking.

Positive thinking is extremely important in holding your confidence and making peace with the world. Positive thinking is making the best of difficult situations, reframing difficult things, completing a grief process, and holding yourself up through it. It is many things. Each of us will have a different relationship with what positive thinking is. There are deep and numerous reasons that you should learn to think positively. Our thoughts affect our bodies in a deeply intimate way. Both go back and forth; the body affects thoughts and emotions in a drastic way. When you learn to develop consistent negative thinking that brings yourself and others down, your entire being is affected in a negative way. Everything from your muscle tensions to your immune system will be weakened by the experience.

Ever heard the expression, "You are what you eat"? There is a variation on that phrase that I enjoy. It goes: "You are what you think." When you think negative thoughts about yourself, you are participating in a sort of self-loathing self-fulfilling prophecy. If you are always telling yourself that you are lazy and worthless, you encourage yourself to do types of behaviors that you consider worthless or lazy. You start to think about yourself as the worst version of yourself. This is something that needs to be battled against. Positive thinking is much better for your overall health. Positive thinking will improve your mood and attention span and even your physical health.

Environment, Belief, and Influence

It starts with a perspective change. You must think about yourself, what do I criticize about myself? Why do I criticize myself? You've got first to identify the ways in which you bring yourself down. This may be an easier process for some than others. Some people have body issues. They don't like the way they look, or they find that they are continually putting themselves and possibly others down for their looks in its extreme—this is known as body dysmorphic disorder. This type of person will need to learn how to do two things: the first is to decide what they want to do, and are actually capable of doing, about their looks. This could be a practice of starting to jog or some other form of exercise. It could involve eating better. Whatever goes down, it just has to be something attainable and gentle. The second task is to let go of anything that you are holding that is negative about your appearance. You can just let that go and say, "I've been exercising lately, which is something that I can do to improve my appearance. That is enough work for me to do in this area," and forgive the rest. You've got to face that voice that is telling you to look horrible and disgusting because that voice is essentially just you. Sometimes, we have bullies or abusive people in your lives, and they tell us cruel things about ourselves. Often, though, it is coming from our own consciousness.

Positive thinking means that you are shifting from the perspective of bleakness and gloominess and starting to acknowledge the beautiful things that you do experience. Oftentimes, it is not that there aren't beautiful experiences in our lives, but rather, we are just not accessing the experiences that are right in front of us. Positive thinking means shifting just a little, from, "Ugh, its dark out today, and I don't want to go to work," to "It's dark out today, but I am going to do my best at work and maybe take a nap afterward." It is not all sunshine and rainbows. A positive thing should be realistic and attainable.

Confidence will be greatly strengthened when you get into positive thinking. Confidence is something that is difficult to measure and difficult to grow. It comes from deep down in the spirit, and it knows that one can be kept safe and sound by his or her own will. Confidence comes from self-security. If there are a bunch of things that you hold in shame, like past experiences, or other sources of embarrassment, you will not find it easy to have confidence. To have confidence, you must let all that stuff go and admit to yourself that you are a person who is worthy of being listened to, hear, and understood, and then communicate yourself that way.

The best and most classic way to be confident is to be yourself and to own it. If you are a tall person, love that you are tall and share it with the world. If you are a short person, own it, and love your shortness. There are all kinds of body traits and all kinds of people who love people with your body traits. Whatever mental or physical traits you might have insecurities about, you just have to give up on those anxieties and let go. It'll be better for you in the long run.

Motivation is extremely important to address for people with depression. Depression is, in large part, very dependent on motivation. The lack of motivation is what drives depression, and oftentimes, this turns into a cycle of lack of motivation and negative feelings. Motivation is a nebulous concept, but we can pretty much say with confidence that when your body is healthier, you are generally more motivated. When you are spending all of your time on addiction or in unhealthy habits, you are feeding this cycle, and your motivation will be cut short. This is unfortunate, but it happens.

A big part of positive thinking is learning to self-talk about good things and also to separate yourself from the bad thoughts. You can just let yourself know that thoughts are not real. You don't have to disprove thoughts; you can just say that they are mean or unnecessary and do away with them. Lots of people out there do place way too much value on their thoughts, and they spend all of their time "strategically" thinking, as to bring out some kind of satisfaction. But the satisfaction never comes.

What is helpful for this situation is to learn how to tell yourself declarations. You are not your thoughts. Your thoughts only exist in your head. Sometimes, they are correct, or true, and sometimes they are not. It doesn't matter. In either case, they do not make you up. You are not a good person or a bad person for what you think.

Thoughts just come through the mind; you don't generate them. Thoughts are a very abstract stream of consciousness that comes through in language or imagery. They are not real. You have the power to make them real; for example, if you have the thought of walking outside tomorrow in the sun, and then you go take a walk outside tomorrow, you have thought of something and then made it real. However, it wasn't real until you did it. Thoughts are not accessible by other people, and they are your own personal psychic space. Now, you need to take care of that space and be able to filter what you want to be a part of that space and what you want to throw out. This is where you can train yourself to have a stream of new, positive thoughts. Start cultivating thoughts that bring you closer to your self-potential. Start rewarding yourself for being nice to yourself and others. Self-care is extremely important.

Positive thinking isn't something that you'll be able to pick up overnight. But if you practice being nice to yourself and being non-judgmental in your thoughts, you can start to make a shift in your thinking. You will find yourself with a more open heart, a wiser mind, and a stronger soul.

Using Psychology to Analyze Others

It can be very difficult to understand why people do the things they do. They might be driven by unconscious drives, or they might be hiding their behavior form the world. It is always impossible to know what a person is doing behind the scenes.

This is why it is very important to stick to what is observable about a person's behavior. If a person is usually about five minutes late, you can know that this is a part of their behavioral patterns, and unless something changes, they will continue always to be five minutes late to everything. At this point, you should not try to change the person's behavior, but rather accept it. If being five minutes late is causing problems, then that is another story. If a person has a habit like this, and it begins to provide others with inconvenience, then a change will have to be made. However, most of the time, you can observe patterns of behavior like this and just let them be.

What does it take to change a person's behavior? Well, in this case, you can just remind the person that they have committed to being somewhere at a certain time, and that they should respect the boundaries of their work item and be there for when it starts. This is if you are responsible for the person's behavior.

If you are not responsible for working with a person, or otherwise have no reason to try to change the behavior, then all patterns must be accepted. This is hard for some people. Some people want everything to work out and be good for them, and they don't know who to accept the world around them.

Acceptance is key here. Accepting behaviors means that you don't judge whatever a person is doing. You can know that their behavior is self-destructive or bad for others, but this doesn't mean that you can't accept their behavior. Acceptance does not mean condoning. What it does mean is that you realize the extent to which you can affect someone else's behavior, and it is really looking at the patterns, which are observable and drawing conclusions from there.

Patterns are observable only in one way to us. It is important not to make assumptions about a person based on their observable behavior patterns. Patterns are merely the data that you have about a person. For example, a person might drink a cup of coffee every morning. Let talk about how much we can surmise just from this one single behavior pattern. One is the aspect of addiction. We can know that this person, judging from this one behavioral trait, has the capacity to be addicted to something. Pretty much all of us do. For example, you cannot judge that this person is an addict and can't keep themselves from doing this. But a cup of coffee in the morning is an addiction.

Patterns can provide you with insight into the motivations of a person. If Sarah usually ends up having out with Mark rather than Jessica, this could be from multiple factors. It could be that Mark is a love attraction for her and that her drive to be in a romantic relationship is more important to her right now than her drive for friendships.

Concentration and attention are important skills to have when you are learning to read people. Your attention and concentration must be firmly affixed to one person in order to read them effectively.

People can be read because people's lives are a story. People go thought individualistic things that make them unique and themselves. Each person has a life story with many chapters, and each person contains multitudes. It is not a question of if you are able to read people, because people will show themselves to you. It is the question of if you will be able to read them and use that knowledge for your own good.

When you are trying to read another person, try to focus all of your attention on them, but while still observing them in a neutral way. Check out their posture. Are they standing up straight? Are they crouched or leaning to one side? This can tell you about the physical state of their bodies. Older people often lean into their posture and will be a bit more hunched over. This is a sign of age. Sitting up straight is a signal that a person is relatively healthy and young.

When people walk, they tend to lead with a certain part of the body. Some people lead with their heads, some lead itch their feet, some lead with the chest. This can give you great insight into the person's drives and how they conduct themselves. A person who leads with the chest may be proud and strong, and they like their physical appearance. If a man has shrugged shoulders that hang down and leads more with the waist, this gives you the idea that they are carefree and laid back. If a woman leads with her hips, it means that she is feeling confident. There are all kinds of ways that body language can provide you with insight into a person's personality.

One of them is how touchy or physically affectionate a person is. Some people like to have hugs the entire life, and they live to connect physically on a basic level in everyday life and conversation. Other people are not so comfortable with physical contact and prefer to eschew hugs for handshakes and a nod of the head. Neither of these is correct, as there is no correct approach to this. You just have to be cognizant of the boundaries that exist, i.e., not hugging a person who clearly doesn't want the physical contact.

The next main point to consider when you are reading people is the affect. What do we mean by affect? The effect is the way that the face is expressing thoughts and feelings. A normal effect is considered one that has a wide range of expressions, for example, smiling when one is happy and having facial expressions that match what one is saying and doing. The affect is a big clue to how someone is feeling. People with some mental illness, for example, have flat affects. This means that their effect does not change very much when they say different things, and they're not able to express feelings with their faces. This comes with a variety of conditions. However, much less severe cases of restricted affect can come simply from being shy or anxious or sad. A person may restrict their effect when they have social anxiety, for example. A person's thoughts can be wildly swinging all over the place, and their face is displaying a neutral, calm reaction. This can be a protective mechanism for some people, for when you hide your emotions, you and other people don't have to deal with the messy reality of where your emotions are. Some people display all of their feelings on their faces. When speed reading people, you just have to determine who much a person's impact is actually representing their feelings. Then, you can engage.

Eye contact is a huge part of this. How much eye contact is the person making? Is it sustained and intimate? Is it broken up? Sometimes, people can be aggressive with eye contact, and it can actually be a way for people to act out their dominance in a situation.

Eye contact is a proximal thing that can connect and divide people. The term Male gaze" was coined to describe the interaction in eye contact or gaze alone. The male gaze is what it is because of the power of the eye. It is something that we often forget, but an eye contact is a powerful tool when you make eye contact with someone, you are making a connection. This connection might frighten some people, and people who are shy or have problems with self-esteem will often avoid eye contact to a high degree. This eye contact is causing this a primal level of connection that they do not trust because they don't trust themselves, and they don't have confidence. A person with confidence is able to make eye contact with anyone they encounter and engage with them. People might be intimidating, but you can always engage with someone in good faith and have confidence in yourself to represent yourself and your ideas effectively.

The only way to start reading people is by practicing. You can give yourself some practice by intentionally putting yourself in a situation where you will be around other people and trying to observe them. Observe their tiny movements, try to see how they hold themselves by looking into their eyes. Do not try and linger, just try to make the interaction as normal as possible, with observing as much as you can about the person.

When you get home, write about it. Try to recreate whatever you saw and observed in the person and try to get every little detail known onto the paper. Try to describe what you saw in that person's emotional state, their effect, their smile or lack thereof, their body language, what words they used, and everything else.

Understanding Where We Come From

When you are looking to read people, you must understand their context. What does this mean? It means knowing the when, where, how, and why they are in the world.

Our cultural upbringing and our family of origin shape us all. The culture that we grow up in has a great effect on our values, our career trajectory, and other realms of development.

If we take the USA as an example of a culture, we can identify certain aspects of it that affect how we are the way we are. In the USA, we tend to be pretty focused on making money. The entire structure of the government is set up to be for the people, but much of it has been corrupted by the purposes of making money. Capitalism is what we strive to live under, but it is a certain kind of capitalism, one that forces us to go to college, choose a job, and live a predetermined path. The reason for this is productivity.

Think about a life where productivity isn't the goal. What would you do? Maybe you would spend more time on art or writing or just observing what is around you. You might spend time on meditation, or just being with nature. Perhaps families would have more time to take care of each other and live happily.

However, we live in a culture that wants productivity above almost all else. Productivity is king; being productive provides money to the big guys. We tend to like youth and beauty in the USA. Once a person is not super young anymore, they become less interesting. The values that are often in older people are similar to wisdom. When a person has reached this age, they tend to learn about the world and start to be able to apply the knowledge they have of the world to their every day and more abstract experience. Youth and beauty are seen as morally good—while being a mess or being old is seen as reprehensible.

We have very strict structures around how people would dress in their country. The rules for dressing well haven't changed much in the last hundred years, and when a person is not dressed in the standard of what we perceive to be normal, we find that to be weird and unattractive. Attractive people are actually seen as more intelligent, even though they are not.

Studies have shown that we ascribe traits to certain people who we find attractive. This could be a movie star or someone walking down the street. Either way, we start to view the person as slightly different for being attractive. Part of this is our animal makeup; evolutionarily, men wanted to find women who would be good mates for raising children, and they looked for youth and body type in their search. Women were attracted to mates who could protect them and who had a social status that would enable them to have a good life. This is a structure of evolutionary psychology that still has remnants in our psychology today. It has absences been co-opted by advertising and corporations, and our need to be attractive overtakes us often. When we see an attractive person, we assume that they are more efficient and smarter than someone who may not be as attractive. This is just one example of who we grow up in a certain culture and start to think in the way of the culture.

We have a male-dominated culture, one that celebrates the accomplishment of men and emphasizes male traits. This can affect women and men in several ways. On the one hand, women tend not to get traded as fairly in the way that they are afforded opportunities and paid in the workplace. The way that this oppression manifests itself in women is in varying degrees. Sometimes, it will include an internalized misogyny and will turn into a stewing heap of resentment. Other women recognize it and work against it. Their struggle to cope with the forces of oppression in their lives will shape the way that there live their lives. Men will also be affected by this society; bemused men are expected to act a certain way. They are expected to be stoic and tough and never show weakness. To share emotions is to be labeled unmanly. They might find that they need to take a special time to learn how to share and express their emotions.

These are all examples of the ways that society faces shape that we are. Peel will have all different types of personalities, no matter their gender or race. But the societal forces that they face will affect the way that their personality is addressed. There are multiple layers that contribute to reading people.

When you are attempting to read people, you should be able to take all of this into account. This means that you should not go from Nebraska and travel to a small island country in the Pacific and expect people to have the same value system as you do. This means recognizing where you came from as a way that you perceive the world and trying to understand that all value systems are objective and that people act how they were taught to act. This might take some time to achieve non-judgmental when you are finding yourself in this problem. Infested of assigning moral good to other groups, try and put yourself in their shoes.

This will require that you use a great deal of empathy, and you will try to learn about a person through the way that they see the world, not the way that you see the world.

There are many different religions, faith systems, attitudes, cultural traditions, and many other differences that distinguish different humans on this planet. However, there are a lot of common connections as well, and there are a lot of ways to understand other people's experiences.

One way to do this is to try food from other cultures. We grow up eating certain kinds of foods, and we usually get used to eating whatever our family ate. This is a great connection woo the world that privies a sense of history and community to the family. This is all great, but it can also be fun to travel somewhere and try to eat the food that they eat on a daily basis. You will start to feel the layout experience the culture a little bit more. There may be restaurants in your town that you have never tired of. Try them, and see how it feels to put yourself out of place every once in a while.

Bias is not something that you should beat yourself up over. In fact, it is a way that you can know yourself more deeply and understand how you are interacting with the world. It can be a painful process to come to terms with your own bias, but ultimately it is something that you will need to face in order to become self-realized. Bias is just a part of the way that we fit into the world.

You also shouldn't convulse your own traditions and values for bias. In our super-woke culture, it is often hip to ignore the old-timey things that our families have done or try to eschew tradition. These people are trying too hard. Traditions are not what hold the bad, regressive views. Traditions need to be upheld; the bad views or olden days can be dropped off without dropping off our culture. Many realize the mistakes of past generations, and they judge them fairly for it. However, we must remember to establish ways that we have cultural continuity and ways that we can come together as a community. The church used to be a placed of the community the church in the USA and has been declining in membership, in most denominations, for many years. This is because people have more access to information online, and they're able to get outside perspectives rather than growing up in a tradition and staying in it lives. Also, people have caught on to the scandals that have been happening in corrupt organizations. The Catholic Church has been mired in scandals of sex abuse for many years. So, people heave goods reasons to leave their churches. What kind of context do we have for the church in 2019? Can it still be relevant?

One thing is for sure, is that the membership of churches is declining, and the churches' function as a pace for community gathering has been largely affected. People just don't use the church to go and see their friends and family as much anymore. This could be seen as a good thing, and it could be seen as a bad thing, but either way, it remains true that we haven't yet been able to establish a replacement for this tradition.

This is a big part of modern life for a young person. They are presented with bad options, such as going to a corrupt church or working for a corrupt job, and then they have to take the options because they don't have any other choices. They are forced to do stuff that they don't agree with backs—there are no other options. What really should happen is young people coming to gather to reform the organizations that they have qualms with and preserving the aspects that are good, like the aspects of community gathering and family-like feelings.

Shyness

Shyness can be caused by a number of things. It could be coming from far back in a person's psyche, or it could just be that they are feeling sick today.

Whatever it is, shyness is the state of not wanting to share what is going on with you into the world. It is a state of not wanting to interact with the world, and not knowing how you will be received in the world. This is a state where you are hiding, within your own mind. It is a state of pride and a state of protectiveness.

You must be kind to yourself when you are a shy person. You've got to engage in polite and kind personal self-talk. For example, you can tell yourself, "It's okay. I'm going to be okay. There will be a few awkward moments, and I will make it through this thing alive." This is the attitude that will help you out. There are thousands and maven millions of shy people in this country. They each have to go figure out their own experiences, but you can know that you are not alone.

One thing to remember with social anxiety is that other people don't really perceive your social situation like you think they do. You might be projecting your own feelings of insecurity, and you might think of yourself as a person who is awkward. The real fact is that everyone awkward sometimes.

Social anxiety may make you feel like you don't want to do anything or go anyway. A big part of learning to deal with this is learning about the anxiety state and learning to modulate your body. The number one way to do this is by breathing. By doing intentional deep breathing, you are able to cause a relaxation response in the body. There are some actions that take intention, like riding a bike or reading. There are other actions that are more automatic, like breathing or blinking your eye. You can, however, decide to do intentional breathing, and you can affect your bodies' physical reaction by doing this. It is a very powerful tool for social anxiety. By employing this tool, you can recognize when your body is going to start to go haywire, and you can go do some breathing to calm yourself down.

If there is an event that you are scared to go to, like a party or a show, you can just notice to yourself as you are approaching the event how you are feeling in your body, and keep checking in every couple of minutes. You will start to notice a tightening, and sometimes it will be in the chest, sometimes in other places in the body. Usually, what is present with social anxiety is a tightening of the chest, a feeling of the heart rate going up, and a feeling of breathing being constricted.

If you are starting to notice that you are feeling the symptoms, just know that you can actually change this at that moment, you can start to breathe, and you will feel differently. Once you start to take some deep breaths, you should notice that your symptoms decrease.

For some extreme cases, this might not be enough. Some people with extreme social anxiety can be diagnosed and prescribed meds that help them to face down these symptoms and go to and be with other people in the world. If you have extreme social anxiety, talk to a doctor, and see if there are options for you to take medication.

Chapter 3: Be Real; Show Your Weakness!

Most people are driven to live happy and full lives. This means that we all have certain innate drives to find ways to live closer and closer to self-actualization. This is a natural state that we find ourselves in as humans. It is an essential part of being humans—we are driven to be better, be stronger, and have deeper connections. However, many things stand in the way of this natural drive. Pathology is one of these things. Pathologies are maladaptive ways that we move in the world. These include disorders of anxiety, emotion, behavior, and thinking. These are the things that get in the way of our happiness. This is what is meant by the phrase "mental health." Our mental health is our ability to cope with the challenges of life and what gives us the ability to live well and be well.

You must consider the context when it comes to the treatment of mental health. We live in a certain time, a certain era. There are stigmas and norms in place. Unfortunately, there is a lot of stigma and shame around mental illness. Stigma is when people place moral judgments on other people for having mental health problems. This might take the form of scoffing or actual joking, or it may be subtler, like subtext in a comment. Mental health issues are sometimes seen as "weak" or "evil" or just embarrassing. This is a huge issue in mental health treatment at the moment. Stigma happens in different ways.

People lack the vocabulary to describe their experiences with mental illness. Someone with the onset of depression for the first time often will not be able to recognize their condition as a medical and mental health one, and may not end up relieving treatment for a long time because they simply didn't understand what was going on. This is caused, in part, by the lack of conversation around mental health issues. When people don't talk about their experiences with mental illnesses in their family, community, or school, it starts to be a subject that is avoided altogether, and this fosters a culture of silence around the issues that matter.

Stigma may be driven by shame for some people. People develop deep senses of worry and shame for their mental health symptoms; this may have come from internalized messages from family or society. People carry shame for a long time; some people never let it get into the light with their issues. They may be afraid that the world will abandon them if they admit they are not perfect, or they may just have a sense of being overwhelmed.

Shame and embarrassment may cause people to avoid identifying their treatment to the outside world. They may tell people that they have a doctor's appointment instead. Some people will share with close friends and family so that they have decided to enter treatment; others will not. When you do share that you are receiving mental health treatment, you are normalizing the treatment and making it more accessible and seemingly safe for others to try. To defeat stigma, a difficult aspect that must be achieved is for people in treatment to start talking about it.

One way to reduce shame and start talking about mental health treatment is to encourage equality between physical and mental illness. When people are diagnosed with diabetes or cancer, a certain respect is typical in regard to the disease. This is not always the case with alcoholism or schizophrenia. We have as humans a natural animal tendency to want to alienate the "weak"; it is a base drive of human nature and must be fought against with morality and reason.

Anxiety is a basic human trait; it has served an evolutionary purpose. Back before civilization was in full swing, our ancestors used to have to be extremely and delicately tuned into their environment. This meant that they had to be ready to defend themselves from predators or other people at a moment's notice. So, our "cavemen" versions had a lot of anxiety, for a good reason, as elephants and stuff were chasing them down. This is all fine and good because it helped to protect them for danger, but we have enveloped since then to have mostly the same anxiety responses, the stimuli are no longer there. There might be times when we need to defend ourselves from animals or other people, but most of sometimes, people's anxiety, which was meant to protect them, is not evolutionarily useful anymore, in terms of their lifestyle and relatively high level of safety, and it just causes disturbances in life. It causes people to be avoidant, to be isolated, and it can cause them to be nervous and shaky in all kinds of situations.

Tips for Making People Feel Comfortable Around You

Anxiety is one of the great problems of the generation of millennials, which is now becoming adults. Anxiety stems from and causes worry. It is a physical state of tension that is often paired with negative thoughts or emotions. Anxiety is a state of being tense and too alert for the situation. Anxiety often comes from worrying about the future or the past, and it often can be paired with other disorders like depression or bipolar.

There are a few things that can help overcome anxiety. One of them is mindfulness. That will be discussed later on. The other is relaxation. Relaxation is an important part of human life, and we often don't acknowledge its worth for our health. Sometimes, relaxation is thought of as an overindulgent thing, but it is necessary and good for our health. There are automatic and manual impulses in our bodily functions. For example, we can bat our eyelids willingly, when we want to wink at a person, but our eyelids will blink automatically when our sensory organs tell them that they are in danger, as well. So, we have voluntary and involuntary responses, and you can use the voluntary ones to "hack" the body into relaxation. Breathing is a great way to use this theory to calm down the body and become more alert and focused and calm. By using deep breathing techniques, you can tap into the response that is provided by extra oxygen going to your brain. You can use that to calm down your body manually. There are studies that show that deep breathing causes a relaxation response in the body. By forcing yourself to breathe slowly in and out, you are able to modify your body's function and slow down what is happening.

Try to make a list of things that you find relaxing. Finding things to relax you is a surefire way to defeat anxiety and get back on your feet.

Procrastination is a nasty habit that gets to a lot of us; procrastination is that little voice that tells you it's cool to do it later. It is a persistent voice, and procrastination has a lot to do with focus. When you aren't able to focus, your mind will get pulled easily from the task at hand. This brings you away from thinking about what you are doing and makes you start thinking about other things. Once you introduce the possibility of doing something else, you will experience a gradual tendency to start to do other things and say that what you started off doing is okay to leave for later.

So how can you start to combat this? Stand up for yourself! Start demanding the focus that you want from yourself. This is a tough job and can lead to strain and struggle, but it will be worth it in the end. You can train yourself to focus; there are some things that you can also do to help yourself along the way. One of them is by eating, controlled amounts. Eat some sneaks every once in a while, to recharge your system and keep you going. Another is by taking breaks. You want to break down your task so that the whole task doesn't feel undoable.

Mindfulness and Influence

One fantastic way to cope with the problems of anxiety, procrastination, and other disorders of thinking and behavior is mindfulness. The concept and practice of mindfulness are rooted in Buddhism. It is an integral part of the path to liberation presented by the Four Noble Truths and the Eightfold Path. Contemporary definitions of mindfulness usually include elements of receptive, present awareness, and striving to forego being reactionary or judgmental.

There is some variance in ideas about the meaning of mindfulness. In some definitions, intentionality is emphasized. In others, there is a greater emphasis on wide and open awareness. Some definitions conceptualize mindfulness as an emotionally neutral process, while for others, like Thich Nhat Hanh, it can be closely linked with positive emotions like kindness or peacefulness. Henepola Guanarantana wrote that mindfulness is extremely difficult to define in words—not because it is complex, but because it is too simple and open. Thich Nhat Hanh, a Vietnamese monk, writer, and activist, describes himself when he is being mindful as being completely myself, following my breath, conscious of my presence, and conscious of my thoughts and actions. A definition of mindfulness which can be useful for consideration in regard to its application in mental health comes from Jon Kabat-Zinn, the developer of Mindfulness-Based Stress Reduction, a program that integrates mindfulness into the treatment of a variety of health conditions. Mindfulness means paying attention in a particular way: on purpose, in the present moment, and non-judgmentally. This kind of attention, Kabat-Zinn writes, can create greater skills of awareness, clarity, and a state of being present in whatever the present moment may be. Meditation can be understood as a formal practice of mindfulness, but mindfulness can be employed in seemingly all life moments and situations.

Mindfulness has influenced trends in psychotherapy in the past few decades in numerous ways. In the area of cognitive-behavioral therapies, there has been the development of MBCT (mindfulness-based cognitive therapy), which incorporates breath work and a perspective of awareness of body, as well as decentering from cognitions or feelings rather than trying to change them. Dialectical behavior therapy was originally fostered as a treatment for behavioral problems, especially people with Borderline Personality Disorder, and was created as a mindfulness-based therapy. It accentuates acceptance skills in the form of mindfulness and distress tolerance. The founder of DBT, Marcia Linehan, developed a schema of a 'divided' mind: the reasonable or analytic mind, the emotional mind, and the wise mind. In DBT, a goal for treatment may be to integrate an understanding of these facets. ACT, or Acceptance and Commitment Therapy, is another example of a contemporary therapy rooted in mindfulness.

You can start a basic mindfulness practice by starting to pay attention to the breath. Just sit in a relaxed place, and calmly let your body let go of its tension. As you sit, just notice how it feels to sit there and feel your body supported by the earth. As you become relaxed, start to shift your attention to the breath. You can pay attention to the breath and how it feels in any way that feels comfortable to you. You might place your attention at the openings of your nostrils, and just feel the cold on the inside the nostril, and the heat of it as the air goes out. You might just put a hand on your stomach and feel it go up and down. Once you have some physical way to pay attention to the breath, see how long you can pay attention to t. At first, the time that you are able to focus may probably be pretty short. This is okay! Beginners are the best for mindfulness. It is all about coming back to your breath. Thoughts will come in; you can just let them leave and go back to the breath. You may feel distracting physical sensations; you may get distracted by sounds or thoughts. All of these will be gone in a few seconds, and you can just put your attention back on the breath.

Once you get a good handle on this, you can transition out of focusing on the breath and not an overall state of awareness. This brings the state of mindfulness to a full-body and sense level, where you are paying attention to each part of your experience.

Mindfulness is a great tool for anyone trying to calm down their minds and get some sense of focus in their lives. Mindfulness can be a turning point for some people. Some people experience a range of whirling thoughts all the time and never learn to deal with it or talk about it until they learn about mindfulness. It gives people a third-person view of themselves, makes them detached and a little bit fairer to themselves and to other people.

The thing is, we spend too much time milling around in our thoughts. Really, thinking can become an addiction in itself. Here, does an experiment: Try to imagine something, a scenario, or an event that occurred. Sit in a chair and close your eyes. Try to feel he temperature of the air in whatever place you are in. Try to see the sights and smell the smells. Try to hear what is happening in the place you are in. Try to feel the ground below you, know that the sky is above you, feel the wind or sound on your face if it is present. Now, snap back to reality. See, our attention is a powerful thing. If you direct it at something, it will go there and stay there. We are able to direct our attention away from things, too. This is how thoughts and feelings become repressed: whenever we experience that thought or feeling, we direct our attention elsewhere and get distracted, and we are able to fix our situation in this way. By repressing, though, you do more damage. Where and when we place our attention is a really impactful thing. If you are always placing your attention on your thoughts, you will be a slave to your thoughts. Your thoughts are not real. Your thoughts are not you. They don't control you; you control your thoughts. There might be times when your thoughts are very intrusive, and they might seem to control you, or even tell you that they control you, but they don't. They are just your thoughts.

Mindfulness has become a phenomenon in the US in recent decades. It is understood as a way to center yourself, to be grounded, and to increase attention, relaxation, and alertness. By starting a meditation practice, you can begin to build your skills of awareness, and grow your insight into your feelings, thoughts, and actions.

Let's talk about what it takes to begin to be mindful. There are some exercises that you can do, which can show you what it feels like to be mindful. Mindfulness engages the senses rather than our cognitive processes. It is part of the idea of focusing on the body, rather than the mind. In our hyper, productivity-cantered culture, people are not encouraged to focus on their senses, but rather to ignore them in order to get work done. By doing some gentle tuning-in to the senses, you can begin to become more mindful of your body. When you tune into your body, you can have a sense of context and insight into your thoughts.

Try sitting in a comfortable position, with your feet flat on the ground, and your spine in a comfortable, lengthened position. You can either close your eyes or have a softened gaze. A softened gaze is directing your eyes about ten feet away, or wherever is comfortable, and allowing them to un-focus, relaxing the eyes, and not making yourself "see" anything or focus on anything. You can also close your eyes, which will give you a different visual experience. You will "see" the inside of your eye. You also might tend to see different patterns, colors, or changing visual stimuli. These are all okay. So, now that you are sitting in a comfortable position, with your eyes closed or in a soft gaze, you can begin just to notice your breath. As you notice your breath, just try to give all of your attention to it. Try to feel what it feels like in your nose or mouth. Try to breathe in through your nose. You can have your mouth closed, or you can relax your jaw completely and sit with your mouth open. This might feel a little goofy at first, but it will allow you to relax your body completely. Focus on the sensation of the breath at the nose or in other parts of the body. You may feel your chest moving up and down, or lower in your stomach. Just try to be kind to yourself as you focus on what it feels like to breathe in and out. You may notice things that you've never noticed before; you may see that parts of your body relax when you take time to put your attention on the breath.

The next step to this is letting thoughts drift in and out. The idea, ultimately, is not to have any thoughts. Pretty radical, right? It is. Don't worry about getting to the supposed endpoint, though; mostly, the people who achieve this are monks or ascetics. It's really about the journey rather than the destination. So, undoubtedly, thoughts will come into your mind while you practice paying attention to the breath. Thoughts will drift in, maybe almost immediately. Don't freak out! What you can do with thoughts is acknowledge that they exist, and let them pass by. You might envision a window, which comes up like on a computer, filling you in with some unnecessary information. Close the window and let it float away. You could think of your thoughts like clouds. Again, let them float through and away. Don't focus on the thoughts; you can just let yourself relax, and all thoughts go away in time. Just bring your attention back to the breath. Every time, you just bring your attention back to the breath.

Mindfulness is not about being perfect or good meditators; it is about coming back. When you come back to the breath, you are bringing yourself back to awareness. This will make mindfulness easier each time you do it.

So here you are, sitting in a relaxed position, noticing the breath, feeling what it feels like on the inside of your nose or mouth, feeling the heat or cold with each breath, feeling the wind. A thought comes up: "I'm tired, and I've got to go to the post office later." It's true. You can just let go of it. It comes into your mind, and you spend a few seconds thinking about it. Then, just let it go and return to the breath. Go back to noticing the body, and the thought will go away. This will provide you with practice so that when disturbing thoughts come up in your consciousness, you can just let them go.

Anxiety and depression come with various symptoms. One that many people do experience is the panic attack. This is when the body is basically shutting down due to panic; it is the body's attempt to reify itself when put in a place of danger. The panic responses that we have are tied to the evolutionary process. If you go back hundreds or even thousands of years, humans developed their emotional and cognitive responses out of the need to survive. The people way back in these times weren't as concerned with traffic laws and getting an A on their exam; they were more concerned about finding food and staying safe from dangerous environments and creatures. They developed anxiety responses that, like other animals, are fight-or flight. When these panic responses are activated, we are taken right back to the land (in our minds and bodies of our ancestors. The same buttons are being pushed now that back then was pushed by the threat of physical danger. Now, we might experience that extreme response when we have something important coming up or have social anxiety around events or other upcoming things in the future. Therefore, we have to account for the animal reactions of our bodies and try to deal with them in the context of 21st-century life.

If you develop a meditation or breathing practice, you can draw upon this experience when you are in times of crisis. Developing your meditation or breathing practice is crucial to the application of them for dealing with physical symptoms like panic attacks.

A panic attack is an episode where you experience great fear; this fear triggers physical reactions. The physical reaction your body has to the danger is what is known as the panic attack. You might feel as if you are losing control or having a heart attack when you are experiencing one of these. Panic attacks are not life-threatening. You cannot die from a panic attack. Sometimes, this knowledge is what helps people calm themselves and get out of the experience. Panic attacks usually include symptoms like a sense of doom, fear of loss of control, increased heart rate, sweating, shaking, chills, or other symptoms.

One of the first strategies that can be used to get out of the panic attack is breathing. By doing deep breathing, we are shifting our focus, getting our body to try to relax, and calming the mind in the process. If you can use breathing in critical situations like having a panic attack, you can slow the onset or decrease the overall severity of the panic attack. The primary function of breathing in this situation is to bring yourself back to a place where you can deal with what is happening. The breathing ifs for grounding, bringing you back to earth.

Another strategy is to tell yourself to stop and think. Your thoughts may be spinning out of control when you have a panic attack. They may be too numerous to count. When you remind yourself to stop and think, you can be directive in what you are thinking about. Rather than having a whirlwind of thoughts, try to direct your thoughts toward the reality of the situation. Remember, this situation is going to be difficult, and there is no magical way to make yourself immediately out of the situation and comfortable again. However, there are some strategies you can employ to deal with the situation more effectively. When you are trying to direct your thoughts, see if you can push them to be positive. You can remind yourself that you are in control, and you can remind yourself of other situations where you had been able to manage panic attacks successfully. You can remind yourself that you are capable and powerful enough to deal with this.

Another way to use your training in mindfulness and meditation is to relax. By relaxing your muscle intentionally, you can sometimes get your heart rate to decrease and your breathing to slow down. You can try all of these techniques whenever is convenient; you may not want to wait for a panic attack to try these out, because then you haven't practiced. Try practicing the scenario in a safe place and time, and then you will have gone through the motions at least once before actually experiencing the panic attack.

Chapter 4: The Power of Fears

Detach from Emotion

When using critical thinking skills, it is important to pay attention to the role that emotion is playing in your decisions. Many of our important decisions will undoubtedly be imbued with emotion. Some of them are relatively easy; others take a great deal of learning and getting through challenges. Oftentimes, we will need to detach from emotions. This chapter is about the situations that drive this need and some strategies to be healthily detached from emotions.

First of all, let's talk about what we're not talking about. When talking about detaching from emotions, we are not talking about becoming cold and disconnected. This can be a source of coping for some people—they become disconnected and "detached" from emotions and use this to be unhealthy and justify it in their minds. This can be described as being aloof. These people are afraid of intimacy and connection. They are afraid of engaging with the world on an emotional level. Of course, we are emotional creatures, and emotions will always be a part of our experience as human beings. We cannot part with this aspect of humanity—thank God. We have to learn to live with our emotions and use them in suitable ways.

True detachment leads not to disconnection and aloofness, but rather to an ability to be wise. Wisdom is described as the ability to use knowledge. Well, detachment helps along the process of wisdom. We cannot use our knowledge if we rely too much on the emotional information that we are experiencing to make a decision. In order to use the knowledge that we have to make decisions and understand our world, we have to contextualize our emotions. Wisdom comes from this contextualization. True detachment involves acknowledging our emotional states and dealing with them in the most efficient manner. When we are detached from emotion, we are able still to engage in emotion while not letting it take over our decision-making.

We've mostly all heard this one before: "When you assume, you make an Ass out of U and Me." This is an important lesson, and understanding ours and other's biases is a big part of not assuming. Like we discussed in the last chapter, understanding biases can help you to realize when you are unfairly assuming something about another person or situation.

The first thing to ask yourself when you are thinking about the reason you assume things are this: Are you a psychic? Do you have a crystal ball that tells the past, future, and present truth? I bet not! You may be a psychic with these powers, and if you are, you should disregard this chapter. For the rest of us, it takes to realize that we are not omniscience and that we can't tell what is going on in other people's minds.

We tend to think of more attractive people as more trustworthy. There are scientific studies that show that people tend to have a bias and assume that people who are physically good-looking have good personality traits, more than we would assume for people who are less traditionally good-looking. Why is this? On its face, it seems totally shallow and ridiculous. There is an explanation, however, for this tendency, if we look to evolutionary theory. People used to choose partners based on physical traits that they felt would ensure their survival. So, it follows that men who were the strongest and fastest would find mates and women who were determined the most physically adapted to take care of children and keep the family functional would be chosen. In men, this led to the propagation of certain traits, and a selectiveness for men who are physically tall, powerful, and muscular. For women, this developed into an idealized mate who had a body that appeared fertile and "womanly." However, we are past that now. We no longer need to choose mates that will defend us from the megafauna of the past. We don't need to choose in this way anymore, but we still have vestiges from the past embedded in our psychology. This has resulted in the expectations of gender that we have inculcated in our population.

Another idea to consider is this: you have no idea what another person is going through. Pain and suffering are subjective. Some people hide their pain from the world. They may present as a happy-go-lucky, content person, but really they have hip arthritis that makes it hard to walk. People may be hiding emotional pain in just the same ways.

Relationship Between Emotional Intelligence and Influence

We can't assume that we know that people are going through how they are feeling internally. Sometimes, we will misinterpret a smile or facial expression. If you have some ideas about a person, like that they are mad at you, you may see the smallest physical move as a move of aggression, or you might find that you interpret their speech too hastily for anger.

How do you stop assuming things? You should analyze your thoughts and see when you are assuming and then try to get to the why of assuming. Why are you doing these things? Sometimes, people start the critical thinking process without having all the facets. They may fill in the information into the process that is untrue; to draw conclusions before they can actually be drawn. You can pay attention to how much our mind is doing this; they try to redirect when you are noticing the assumptions. You might find that you have some biases that you had now acknowledged before.

There are three ways of thinking to consider when you are analyzing your thinking. The first is the emotional mind. This is the mind that makes decisions under duress and will be only taking into account the data that is coming from the emotions. The emotional mind will be frenzied, whirling, and unstoppable. It will be passionate and driven by love, art, humor, and romanticism. The next way of thinking is the logical mind. The logical mind is driven to make decisions without any source of emotional data whatsoever. The logical mind can ignore a crying face. It can deny emotion and prove to the world that it has never felt anything, ever. It was a way to self-denial that can be very satisfying for some people. Most people don't make decisions this way, but some do. The logical mind is not good at understanding people in a whole way; it totally relies on scientific observations and quantifiable data. The third and more moderate way of thinking is the wise mind. The wise mind takes into account both the emotional mind and the logical mind when it is making decisions. It addresses the problems of emotionality and the problems of logic. It takes input from both of their perspectives; if the emotional mind is saying something, it listens and responds gently. If the logical mind is making its case, it weighs the importance of logic in that situation. The wise mind is a beautiful synthesis of these two forms of human awareness. It is called the wise mind because it embodies the wisdom that we see in the most intelligent and efficient people. Oftentimes, you will find that older people have more wisdom. This is not true for all older adults, but a lot of them. They have acquired more wisdom simply because they have had more practice in making a decision. Over and over again, they have made decisions. Maybe sometimes, they had let their emotional minds take over their decisions, and they saw how that played out. They have also witnessed the ravages of the logical mind, a mind that is disconnected and aloof, and seen the effect that that way of thinking has on their decisions. Often, older wise people are known as "not giving a damn."

Simply, put, they don' sweat the small stuff. They have a perspective on life that is influenced by having lived through most of it. They know the importance of emotions, but they also know not to get too wrapped up in it.

Let's face it: it's great to live in emotions. It can be a very indulgent thing. Some people can even enjoy the melancholy sadness that comes with depression; it becomes a certain flavor to your file. There is a certain sweetness to depression, and it can be satisfying, especially for artists and creative's, to live in this sadness and relish it. It feels food for them to be sad. It sounds concerned, but that is the way that we adapt to our lives sometimes. Other people may be more comfortable with the emotion of anger; they will find themselves resorting to angry actions or words to get their point across or get things done. These emotions are states that we hold on to because we feel that they will help us somewhat. Outside of normal emotional functioning, however, there exists the other side to the story— the logical mind. The logical mind works with reason and practicality. If you find yourself having trouble detaching from emotion, try embracing the logical mind. The logical mind is what you use when you are scheduling things, doing at problems, or planning a trip by calculating gas mileage. It doesn't need any emotional input to make decisions. However, you must remember that the goal is not to become disconnected and aloof, but rather just detached. Healthy detachment is necessary.

Some people will stand in your way when you try to detach from emotion. Some people want to see you wound up, to see you emotional because they want you to continue the patterns of behavior that you have been engaging with before. Change is hard for people to accept. The people who react negatively to someone being more detached from emotion do negatively react because they are bad people, but because they are people with fears, desires, wants, and needs like the rest of us. This should not, however, stop you from changing your mindset and behavior in order to detach from emotion more thoroughly.

You see, we each have patterns of thinking, feeling, and behavior. Our patterns get interwoven with the people around us. This can happen in positive and negative ways. For example, there may be someone you often see who you like. They say hi to you, you say hi to them, and you feed off of each other/ energy. This is a great way to have an interpersonal relationship—simple, easy, and low-pressure. Another way we get intertwined with people is in our intimate relationships. When we are dating or married to someone, we have a different set of ways that we interact with him or her. For one, you may have a sexual relationship with this person. You may be more honest with this person that you are with other people. You might find that yon your relationship with them, you are subject to each other's needs, even physical needs, more often than other people are subjected to them. This is fine and good. Sometimes, however, we get used to accommodating our partner or spouse's need too much, and we take on negative behaviors that accompany or complement others' bad habits. Here's an example: Jane has three sisters. They are loud, boisterous, and fun. She is the youngest. As Jane is halfway through high school, she gets her first boyfriend her sisters all give her lots of teasing about it and make fun of her from "K-I-S-S-I-N-G" in the tree and all of that. So, this is her first stressor: she feels pressure and anxiety from her sisters, who like to point out a relationship that is new and unknown in her life. Her new boyfriend, Dan, is a sneaky guy. Jane is attracted to Dan's "bad boy" status and often is seen accompanying him on his cigarette breaks outside of school, even though she doesn't smoke. Dan likes that Jane comes with him on his smoke breaks, as he, after all, does feel a little unhealthy and ashamed about his habit. So, when Jane starts to be more reluctant about being around Dan when he is smoking, Dan reminds her that, "I feel lonely out there, and I don't want to be alone." Jane starts to stay with Dan consistently, and eventually, she picks up the habit for herself. Jane's parents notice her new habit, and they are not happy. They have a long talk with Jane, and they tell her about the risks associated with smoking. They tell her about addiction and about how cigarettes work in the body. Jane understands all this and is convinced that smoking isn't for her. Even though she likes Dan, and wants to be his girlfriend, she doesn't want to smoke. So now Jane has a big problem: first, she has to deal with the teasing of her sisters, but now, she has to deal with the teasing all while starting to modify her behavior. Dan approaches her after lunch on the following Monday and asks her to come outside with him to smoke. Jane decides that she doesn't want to do this anymore, and she tells Dan just that. He starts to go on his diatribe about how lonely and sad it is to be let alone during these times, and Jane starts to feel a little sad for him. She stops, however, and detaches from her emotions. She says to Dan, "I'm sorry that you feel lonely. I have made a personal decision for myself that I don't want to smoke, because of the health risks, and I won't be joining you on smoke breaks anymore. I still like you and want to keep dating." Dan storms off in a huff. However, later, when he thinks it through, he realizes that Jane was honest and mature in her statement. He is able to accept this about Jane and even thinks about quitting smoking himself.

Making Adjustments

If you are to adjust and change to make the happiness that you deserve in life, you've got to start taking a realistic view of yourself. For some people, it may take focusing on their limits; they might realize that they aren't all that they puffed themselves up to be in their minds. For many people with depression, the goal is to battle negative thoughts. Automatic negative thoughts are very common in anxiety and depression, and these must be pushed back against so that a person can have acceptance. A person must acknowledge that they deserve love and that they are good how they are. Now, this does not include denial; if a man is an addictive gambler, and never acknowledges the pitfalls of his behavior, this is not an example of a person who has wholly accepted him or herself. It is a picture of denial. In most cases, however, a person with depression and anxiety can do some work in the self-esteem area. This involves taking an inventory of your strengths and weaknesses. If you look closely, you can find some ways that you are individually very strong and talented. Everyone has special ways that make him or her adapted to challenges. People are interesting! This means you are probably interesting. One way to work on acceptance of how you are and how you want to be is by writing about it. Try writing the story of your life. Doing this has many benefits. For one thing, it can provide clarity. Sometimes, our thoughts stay stuck in our heads, rotating and bouncing and flying around, sometimes coming back and back again. When you put these onto paper, it can make things a little easier to deal with. Now, you are not working with abstract ideas that cannot be found materially. You have some external material to work with and interpret. Telling stories is how humans communicate. Once you start to tell your story, you will notice how you tell it. If you are telling your story with love towards yourself, and joy in the world, you will find that your story is accurate, fair, and uplifting. Many will find that the stories they tell themselves and others about their life are inaccurate in some way or overly harsh.

Start at the beginning: where did you grow up? What kind of family life did you have? It is fair and sometimes necessary to revisit your context to examine why you might be experiencing the problems that you are experiencing. Maybe you grew up with a family that punished the expression of emotion; maybe you grew up in a family who was overly emotional and had trouble regulating the emotions in the family. These details can help you to figure out who you are and why you are. Most of the time, when you really apply fairness and kindness to your analysis of your child's self, you will find that you were just doing your best to adapt to the challenges you were experiencing.

Going on from there, what were your early school days like? Did you have trouble separating from family life? Do you remember having friends at this age? At each stage, it is important to keep an open mind and be kind to yourself and others in your analysis.

Another factor to consider in your story is the cultural context. Maybe you grew up in the Midwest US. Maybe you grew up in a country outside the US, and you moved somewhere else. These are part of your timeline and are details that matter.

What you are trying to do by telling your story is to give yourself a little bit of control over the narrative. People with depression or anxiety may feel that their symptoms are out of control. By telling your story, you can see where and why the problem arose and how to go forward with treatment. The treatment is not for you to become a good boy or good girl, but rather to bring you to a pace of happiness and healthiness that lets you reach the potential you have as a person. People don't like being anxious and depressed, and it is not the natural state of being for people. You must acknowledge that you are well and good as a person, but that you need treatment for an illness that you have.

Okay, so we've talked a little bit about how you can relate to yourself, but now let's talk about relating to ourselves in relation to others. Did you get that? Put more simply: Don't give a crap about what other people think or say. That belongs to them, and not to you.

Sometimes, people have the problem of projection. This means that they are taking feelings and thoughts that exist in their own heads and "transplanting" them into the heads of others. This is an illusion, obviously, because we cannot tell what others are thinking, and we certainly make them think of any certain thing because of the thoughts existing in our heads. Take, for example, any standard insecurity. Let's say that Rachel is very self-conscious about her legs. She is wearing a dress that shows more of her legs than she is accustomed to, and she is going to a party where she will be around many of her peers. Rachel's anxiety kicks in, and she starts to think, "Everybody is going to see my legs and find out that I'm horribly unsexy." She thinks this but gathers up enough courage to go to the party anyway. Rachel doesn't realize that she is a whole person, with strengths and faults, and she is very judgmental about her body. She doesn't realize that she doesn't have to be judgmental about her body. Rachel ends up going to the party, and people notice different things about her. One person notices her red hair and gives Rachel a nice compliment about it. One other person thinks that they have seen her around, possibly at the coffee shop they both used to frequent. Not one person thinks in their mind that Rachel's legs are anything but normal, if not attractive. See what's going on here? Rachel has totally lost sight of the big picture and has told herself a story about other people and herself. The story is this: I am a gross person because my legs look a certain way, and people always notice and find it unattractive. There is nowhere in reality that this is even close to true. These are just stories we tell ourselves when we are trying to deal with the world.

Differentiation is a process that happens when we are young children. There is a lot of research out there about parenting and the early years of childhood development. This is a time when the child must establish a permanent, trusting, deep bond with the mother, and father, and then at a certain point, start to understand themselves as a different person than their parents. At the very beginning, as is the mystery of life, we are fused with another person – literally part of another person. As we enter the world, we begin to exist independently in our own bodies. But that link is still there. After a while, a person learns to develop intimate relationships and also be very independent. This is what a generally well-functioning person is able to do: have very close moments of intimacy, long-term relationship with intimacy, and also be confident in oneself, able to take care of oneself, and to be able to tolerate long periods of independence.

Some people have more trouble with this than others. Parents may notice that their child's attachment is insecure or avoidant; they might recognize their child pulling away at certain times or never wanting to be without the parent. These can be signs that the child has not developed a sufficiently mature level of differentiation.

As another example of differentiation, let's take high school as an example. High school kids tend to love fads and to go with the latest "cool" thing, whether it is a movie, music, type of shoes, or whatever else. Let's say that at a certain high school, there is a new Superman movie out. It gets out that this is the coolest movie experience of the year, and everyone "must" see it. Their peers are influencing them, and many will end up watching the movie, whether or not it is a good movie. There tends to be safety in numbers, and people inherently understand that. So, when George, a 10th grader who has exceptional taste in film, says at the lunch table that he respectfully did not enjoy the new superman movie, and is able to express his opinion calmly and with an open mind, he is demonstrating a high level of differentiation for his age.

Another thing that comes along with differentiation is honesty. It takes confidence to be honest. If you are always worried about what other people are going to think about our personal preferences and habits, you will find yourself very alienated.

The opposite of differentiation is co-dependency. This is a behavior and relationship pattern. Sometimes, it is passé down through generations. It is a condition that affects your ability to have a healthy and mutually satisfying relationship. It can be known as a sort of relationship addiction. Usually, people who are co-dependent end up in relationships that are one-sided. These relationships may be destructive or abusive. This kind of relationship can be common in families affected by alcoholism or addiction. Co-dependency can affect spouses, parents, siblings, friends, or co-workers. The phrase originally comes from describing the dynamics in families with addictions. You can also see this pattern, however, in families that have not experienced this. It becomes a way of being in the world.

Something that many people will find that they need is self-forgiveness. Admit your sins, and laugh about it! First of all, take into account why you made bad decisions. This might go back a little bit to the acceptance topic. When you look back on things that you have done that you know that was wrong, ask yourself, what would you tell a good friend if they have done what you did? There is a good chance that you will help them to understand that what they have done is forgivable and that they will be able to find a way forward. Ask yourself what that voice is. That voice says things like, "It's okay not to be perfect." In fact, it's impossible to be perfect, so you can just give up that pursuit right away.

You might find that you are holding grievances toward others but also towards yourself. These are things that people need to learn to let go of. This may mean thinking, it may mean talking to a therapist, it may mean writing, or walking alone contemplating. Whatever it takes, you need to let go of the grievance against yourself. You can look at this through the lens of forgiveness of others as well as self-forgiveness. Let's say that Dan, your friend, hit you in a rear-end fender bender years ago. It was his fault, and he profusely apologized. However, the brazen way that he did this always got you thinking about Dan's true intentions. Did he just not care at that moment? Could Dan have done this on purpose? How can you trust him? We will hold on to these unanswered questions for years. Later, down the road, we will still be thinking about how Dan did us wrong and why we can't trust people now. The reason you need to let go of this is not for Dan. Dan has since moved on and doesn't' even remember the incident anymore. You need to forgive Dan for yourself.

Therefore, you can apply this own process to your own misdeeds. It can be helpful in this process to talk with a professional counselor or therapist. They might be able to assist you in processing events from the past with skill and helpfulness. As you revisit parts of your past, it can be good to have another person there to remind you that you are not a bad person and to point out inaccuracies in your thinking. Those of us with depression and anxiety will have a lot of inaccuracies in our thinking about ourselves. We tend to think of ourselves as less-than, or weak, or sick. Other people might have a completely different perspective; they may be thinking that our lives seem fascinating and adventurous and even amazing. We are not able to see this ourselves because of the conditions that we are facing.

This book is centered on the radical change that will need to take place in three weeks in order to change the situation that people with depression and anxiety find themselves in. This will take a lot of courage and a lot of kindness. For people who are not good at forgiving themselves or others at first, and find it uncomfortable, there is the option of trying out a type of meditation. This specific meditation deals with sending positive energy out into the world to various entities and people. The meditation usually involves reciting some kind of message in your mind, like "may you be happy, may you be healthy, may you have peace," while we think of a person or entity. There are different ways to do this, but one way is to picture someone you care a lot about, and who it is easy to feel love for them. Choose someone who is a benefactor, a person who has helped you out in your life, like a parent or trusted friend or teacher. Picture them in your mind, think about how much you love them, and send out the message: May you be happy, may you be healthy, may you have peace. Think this over and recite it in your mind, maybe five times. Then, pick someone else, who you tend to take care of. This could be an animal, or a child, or someone who is dependent on you for you to take care of. Think towards them: may you be happy, may you are healthy, may you have peace. Then, think about someone you have been having a difficult time lately. This could be someone who you recently were fighting with or someone you have been holding a grudge against. Think about them, you don't have to linger if it is too uncomfortable, but think about them and send out the message: may you be happy, may you be healthy, and may you have peace. Finally, think of yourself. Try to extend the loving kindness that you have for others towards yourself. This will help to prime your sense of kindness by practicing with others before you turn the forgiveness on yourself. That will break down the resistance that many people experience in this process and let you see yourself a little more objectively.

There is another exercise that you can do to help yourself get out of your subjective experience and enter a feedback loop with the world, a sense of being and belonging. This exercise involves thinking about yourself in the third-person. If your name is Brenda, think about what you have done so far today. "Brenda woke up, had a little bit of a hard time getting out of bed, and took a shower." You can start with seemingly trivial parts of your day. It might be your daily routine or commute; you might describe your meals. By doing this, you remove yourself from the limited perspective of just being in your own head, and you start to think about yourself as a whole person. This technique will let you compare your thoughts to the reality of the situation. First, write down your thoughts about what happened. It could be, "I went to the grocery store and bought chocolate like I always do because I'm a dirty addict." This is a little exaggerated, but God knows that people do think this way about themselves sometimes. Then, write down what actually happened: "Mark went to the grocery store, got tempted, and bought some chocolate." This is a kinder, more accurate description of what happened. It tells the truth, nothing more or less.

Chapter 5: Build Empathy with the Right Narrative

Most people are good, right? Maybe you are the type of person who believes that most people aren't good. This is an argument that has gone on for centuries—the innate goodness, or lack thereof, in humans. Perhaps if we had a perfect society, there would be less impetus to be able to read and analyze people. However, even if everyone in the world were trustworthy and essentially good, that still wouldn't mean that it is not important to be able to analyze people. Wanting to be free from the danger of someone manipulating you is a good reason to want to be able to analyze people, but there are also other reasons.

Parents, for example, have to learn how to analyze behavior when they are raising children, as this allows them to read into the lives of their children and really get a sense of their well-being. Therapists and other healthcare professionals need to analyze people in order to help them. Teachers need to be able to analyze people to assess where they are in their learning in order to determine where they need to be. Even if you don't work in one of these professions, though, it is still important for you to be able to analyze people. Why? The short answer is that it makes life easier. It makes it easier for you to achieve what you want to achieve. It makes it easier for you to get through your day. It makes it easier to form lasting relationships and know which people to avoid.

Social Influence and Defense

It is important to be able to protect yourself. There are so many people in the world who fall prey to all sorts of scams and manipulation. We'd love to think that everyone in the world has great intentions, but that is not the case. The most vulnerable people in society tend to get scammed the most. Just think of the classic phone scammer situation. Phone scammers love to try and get in touch with older people, who are not as familiar with technology or might be out of touch with the processes of modern society. They make good targets to be manipulated because of this. People tend to see weakness and exploit it. The bad guys out there aren't looking for the toughest, sharpest people to exploit; rather, they are looking for the ones who will be easy.

This is the simple and brutal truth, and the way that you can help yourself and help others is by being more aware of people and being able to analyze people. When you are able to read into others' behavior, language, and body language, you can decode some of the messages that you are receiving, and you can learn more about people quickly. This may end up in many ways. Maybe you will be able to tell that they are good-hearted and have only good intentions. Or, you might find that you are able to save yourself or someone else from a whole lot of inconvenience.

We all have a capacity for intuition. What is intuition? Well, it is a difficult thing to describe. It is a feeling, which we interpret into words, which comes from some part of our psyche. Intuition is a physical, emotional, and cognitive process that happens all at once, and it affects nearly every decision we make. Intuition is a very nebulous and esoteric concept. Intuition is something that comes from our core, and it has a lot to do with morality. It tells us what we think we should be doing deep   down.

Intuition is very important for analyzing people. It can be thought of as the foundation for reading people. Information is important, and you can learn a lot about analyzing people from outside sources, but what it is going to come down to is learning to trust your intuition and really find a way to learn from yourself.

Communication is another part of why it is important to learn to analyze people. Communication is one of the most important skills that people will need to learn to function in this world. It is so important that people who can't learn to communicate often get shut out of society, even if it is unfair—when you are able to read and analyze people, all of a sudden, some of the questions that you would've needed to ask before become unimportant. This is because you can already tell what is going on with the person before you start talking.

Analyzing people can give you the ability to predict what is going to happen and anticipate it, rather than having to wait and see. When you are not able to analyze people, you will find that you have to take more time to learn about people, and you don't have the immediate ability to see where problems and solutions are.

Analyzing people can also let you learn about yourself, and, indeed, learning about yourself will be a big part of the process in order to learn how to analyze others. Self-awareness is the skill of being able to see yourself objectively. This works in accordance with analyzing others. When you are able to analyze yourself, and see patterns, it strengthens your ability to see patterns in others, and it helps you to develop a base of knowledge around behavior.

Finally, analyzing others can be seen as a spiritual pursuit. The pursuit of knowledge in this area is one of the most personalizing and emotional pursuits; when you learn to analyze people, you learn to be a better person. You start to think about your values, what you think is right and wrong, how you perceive others, and what you want to be.

The first relevant skill that will be discussed here is neutral thinking. Neutral thinking is different because we tend to get wrapped up in all sorts of experiences and thoughts. Thinking objectively about ourselves may take some practice. When you learn to think objectively, you will be noticing what your thoughts, feelings, and behaviors are without being judgmental.

In order to progress as a person, we must learn that we are not our thoughts. Your thoughts are not you. They don't represent you as a person. They are independent of you. Thoughts are not something that you try to happen; they are automatic. You must just learn to ride the wave of your thoughts. This will require that you sit back and relax and just watch your mind like a TV. See what is on the television as it flips through channels automatically. It will go from here to there, from yesterday to tomorrow. The mind will be all over the place, sort of offering different scenarios for you to think about, and you get to decide what you pay attention to. You can practice dealing with various thoughts by just seeing them come into your consciousness—as if through a window, floating, and then coming back out of the window and leaving your consciousness.

This visualization can help you to realize that your thoughts are separate things from you and that they're floating out in the spheres, but they are not actually real. This is something that most people don't realize: that thoughts are not real.

If you take a minute to consider the complexity, you will realize that our thoughts are an incredibly abstract concept. It is when we are using language that we had to learn, to spontaneously develop content, in our heads, using our voice, only to ourselves. It is something that you can definitely take time to trip out on if you'd like. Just take a while and think about the wonder of consciousness. Consciousness basically means human consciousness, not animal consciousness. The human version is something that is the most wondrous tool that we know of in the universe. The human mind is something that is so great and vast that it has created civilizations accounted for the force of incredible good and devastating evil. The mind is not quantifiable at all; it only exists in the abstract. Certain methods can quantify behavior or brain chemicals or some parts of brain function.

Reading Minds

Just think about that: you can never actually know what another person is experiencing. They can describe it to you, but, as we will discuss, language is a blunt force tool, and may not always be accurate. All of the descriptions and quantification in the world cannot accent for this basic separation. It is the separation that makes us human and drives the need for individualism.

The next major tool that we will discuss is listening skills. Developing listening skills is a very important tool for analyzing people. When we are talking about analyzing people, we are talking about the ability to understand others, and what better gift to have when trying to understand others than to listen to them? Listening skills give us a key into other people's lives, and to have that key is a responsibility as well as a privilege. You must treat others with respect and don't abuse the power that comes along with being a good listener.

A person who is a good listener can go through an entire conversation with minimally speaking or asking questions.

They may be able to guide the conversation along without saying anything at all by suturing their body language. They might be so preoccupied with listening to the person that they don't feel the need to talk at all. Depending on whom mocha a person needs to talk about and how bad they deed to talk about it, this can vary from person to person.

Developing listening skills can be the difference between being a poor communicator. A good communicator can sum up all that the other person has said. A person who is good at communication will be a good listener because they know how to absorb the information with strength and attention to detail. Communication depends on the interflowing words between two people. There must be a circle-type feedback loop between two entities to develop strong communication.

Listening skills are when you feel a certain way about someone. Can you remember a time when you felt held, and loved? It might be a parent or a school teacher or counselor or someone else. That is what a really great listener can do. They can make you feel smart. They can make you feel like you are participating and angering with them in a fair and good level. People like to be seen and heard, and you can give people a surprising amount of validation by just paying attention to them.

Being able to do this for people, then, is an indispensable skill. Therapists have to learn how to be impartial observers to whatever is happening. When a person is listened to, they feel themselves in the world, and they feel its transformational powers.

In fact, many of the people who go to therapy for some other reason think they have some large need for therapy in one area realize that they just needed attention and love and to feel like they are listened to. People will go to therapy, not realizing this, and session enfetter session—if the therapist is a good one, they will find themselves feeling better just by having talked it out. Some people crave being listened to ant they never get it.

It is hard to ask for what you need, and sometimes it can help just to ask to be listened to. Sometimes, you need to find someone who is a professional to help you along. Ultimately in order to develop listening skills, you have to be a person who is interested in the world and interested in other people. You need to be a person who likes to find out why people do the things they do, and you most are a person who likes to bring joy to people.

Another important tool for self-awareness and analyzing others is journaling. Journaling is an excellent way to externalize thoughts and feelings. When you have acquired experiences, those thoughts and feelings that are associated with experiences start to build inside you. You have a choice. You can express them or keep them repressed. The first choice is the better one because to keep repressed feelings in for so long is never sustainable. Repressed feelings find ways to leak out of the system in many other ways, whether it be unexpected aggression or acting out in other ways.

Journaling gives you a chance to say what you need to say out in to the world. Some people will find this more difficult than others. Journaling gives you some distance between you and your thoughts, which is necessary because to be able to observe something, you must be outside of it. It's hard to give measurements of the fishbowl when you are a goldfish swimming around in it. Journaling makes our thoughts seem less crazy and less out there and gives us a chance to see what we what to be like. Some people will find that journaling freely is easy. Some won't.

Free-journaling is a great skill that you can learn to practice. At first, give yourself five or ten minutes to just write whatever comes out. Don't filter it; try not to stop. It doesn't have to be related to any single topic; you just need to let the words flow. This is incredibly challenging to do honestly, and it will be a fight to keep it up for longer than five minutes at first. However, writing is like a muscle, and the longer that you flex it, the more you will be able to journal about your life successfully and easily.

Journaling is a great example of what analyzing people is all about: exploring, looking, investigating, trying to think critically about oneself, in the hope of ultimately understanding oneself to the degree that you can apply yourself in the world to the way that you desire. Emotional intelligence is both about being logical and having reason and science behind you, but it is also about the raw experience of experiencing everyday emotions and thoughts, from the very mundane to the deepest depths of human expression.

Journaling can be both. BF Skinner was a famous psychologist who came up with the concepts of behaviorism. Behaviorism is a strain of psychology that emphasizes looking at things in a measurable way. An example of a study in the style of behaviorism would be something like training a horse to run a lap for a carrot. Each time, the behavior is reinforced by the treat. This type of psychology lets you treat everything like a science experiment, and this is a great way to get some empirical data on your problems.

You can try to incorporate the principles of behaviorism into your journaling by taking data about yourself and analyzing it. If you want to go full-on scientific method, you can develop a hypothesis and test it. Your hypothesis may be something like; I will exercise more if I eat breakfast every day. Then, in your journal, record how many times in a week you exercise, and how many of those days you ate breakfast. From there, you can do further testing and learn your patterns of behavior and get to where you want to be. This will make you feel like an amateur scientist, and that's okay because it is good to be your own scientist sometimes.

Mindfulness for Defense

Again, the tool to help with this is mindfulness. This helps you tap into your intuition. Mindfulness is awareness, in the present moment, without judgment. Mindfulness is paying attention to whatever the object of the mindfulness is—this could be thoughts, it could be feelings, and it could be bodily sensations. Whatever the object of your attention is, you use that to practice focusing your mind for small periods of time, and then work up to larger amounts of time. Mindfulness ultimately refers to the integrated awareness of every experience in the woody, whether it is bodily sensations alone, or if there are other aspects of the experience that pop up. These could include smells, sights, or whatever else. The ultimate goal is to get to a place where your mindfulness captures your entire expertise at any moment. This will take lots and lots of work.

The way to start a mindfulness practice is to start by paying attention to the breath. The breath has several physical qualities. It may have a sound. It may just be detectable by feeling the bodily sensations in your chest and nostrils. It may have other qualities, other textures that you can pay attention to. It is also a rhythmic phenomenon, which makes it a great way to tune in to the body.

When you start, just take a second to get comfortable and find where you want to sit for a minute. When you have found a place to sit or lie down, then you can just start paying attention to your breathing and focus your attention all over the breath. Each time you inhale, try to feel it in your nostrils or belly, and when you breathe out, try to feel it then as well. When you are doing this, your thoughts will come into your consciousness.

This is okay and to be expected. When you experience thoughts, just let them go away. You can acknowledge that they exist, but then you can just return your attention to the breath. This becomes a cycle of getting distracted and then coming back to the breath, and this is the way that you can start to develop a practice of paying attention to the body. One exercise to try when you are starting out to number each breath. When you breathe in, count 1. The exhale does not have to be counted. When you breathe in again, count 2. Then, you just continue as far as you want, or you can start over when you get to ten. This will give you a way to connect to each breath and make sure you are paying attention to each and every moment that you are experiencing the breath.

This practice has a profound effect on the body. As you start to pay more attention to the body, you will find that you are able to be more present in your life. See, most of us have the problem of lending too much credence and too much importance to our thoughts. Our thoughts are not voluntary, they are just something that happens to our bodies and minds, and it is something that we just need to learn to cope with as human beings. It is not something that you should judge yourself for. People start to care a lot about their thoughts. This might take the form of worry when a person is always concerned about the future for the past. This might take the form of over-analysis, where a person is not able to just enjoy things without spending too much time thinking about it. It might lead to a person not being able to connect with other people, and being too much in their head when they should be with another person.

Mindfulness practice fights giant this imbalance and helps us to be more integrated individuals. It does this by helping to train you to learn to be a more in-the-body person than an in-the-head person. This will also lead to more emotional intelligence, where a person is able to tell more about their emotional experiences. The emotional experience is something that happens in the body. It is not a thought event, but rather a physical event. So, you can pay more attention to your emotional experience by paying attention to the body, and this will lead to a higher level of awareness.

You might ask how a higher level of awareness can lead to an increase in your ability to read people. Well, if you think about what it takes to read people, you will find that an awareness of self is important. It lets you know that when you feel angry with a person, you are actually angry, and you can have more confidence in yourself that you are expressing the emoting that is what you want to express. You can trust your gut more when someone tells you something that might not be true. You can be more in touch with your experience with other people, and they will be able to trust you to be an authentic person. Just by being more authentic, you will be able to read people easier because it is something that draws other people out.

Intuition

Intuition is an abstract concept. There is no way to study it, except to ask someone to describe their experience of intuition. Intuition is a combination of your spiritual self, your physical self, and your cognitive self, all coming together. It takes into account the feelings that you are experiencing, the thoughts, and the bodily sensations that you are experiencing, and it tells you what feels right at the moment.

Intuition is a deeply human thing that is not explained easily. It isn't anxiety, it isn't a fear, and it is not an emotion. Rather, it is a combination of emotion and thought and sensation that leads you to be able to make decisions. When you are feeling your intuition, try to follow it. Some people don't know what it feels like to be able to follow their intuition; they might not even be aware when they are getting the hint about something or somebody.

Intuition is that little feeling that this person is lying to you, or that slight drop in the gut when you realize that you've won a prize. It is your body reacting before your mind can. The body's really an intelligent construction; we like to think of the minds the source of intelligence in the west, but that's only partially the case. The body is to thank for some of our peer feeling and intuitive processes, and the body is what tells us when we are in danger when we are being lied to, when a person needs genuine help, or when we are in love. A mind is a place that is filled with tight thoughts and ideas. The body is filled with actual sense data that is more trustable than thoughts.

Think about the last dream that you had. Were you aware that it was a dream? Probably not. There are some people who have reported that they are able to control their dreams, in a process called lucid dreaming. In this process, a person is able to point out to their sleep consciousness than they are experiencing a dream, and that what they are imagining is not actually real. When they are able to do this, people can then direct their actions in the dream. They can start to be more in control, and they can find a way to be aware of their dreams. Most people do not have this skill, however, which is perfectly normal. To them, it seems like their dreams are completely real. When they are experiencing dreams, they are not able to distinguish from reality, and even though that content of the dream may be fantastical and unrealistic, they find themselves believing that everything in the dream is true and is actually happening. This just shows how unreliable our minds are. If they are able to construct a whole new reality where you can fly or do other things that are completely unrealistic, then just imagine how far off you can get in your thinking in everyday life.

The body is not so fallible. The body doesn't think; it just reacts. The body is a place where you cannot control what is happening, and that is where the truth comes in. The truth is in body language because the body just reacts. There is no cognitive filter process.

When you feel a certain way about a person in your intuition, just try to see that that is valid. It may not be something that you want to act on, but you can start to realize that your bodily feelings of intuition are valid, and then you can start to do something with them. Many people grow up learning to ignore their intuition for various reasons. One such reason is that they were encouraged not to express emotions when they were younger. Many younger people with strict parents are like this; they are shown or told when they are kids that expressing emotions makes them weak and that they should not express emotions for fear of being abandoned or criticized. This is a very damaging way to grow up, and it affects a person's ability to be able to trust their intuition. For a person like this, confidence will be the key to developing the ability to trust the intuition.

This is a person with low self-esteem. A person with low self-esteem will have trouble trusting their instruction because they have either learned or told themselves that their gut is not something to be trusted. This is not the case, because, for everyone, his or her inner feelings are valid. So, this person will have to learn confidence. Exposure therapy is good for this; the principles of exposure therapy state that when you are exposed to something that you are uncomfortable with for an extended period of time, you will start to learn how to deal with it more, and you will start to be able to withstand periods of exposure to the stimuli more because you are able to take the heat, so to speak. This means that people with confidence issues should look to put themselves in places outside of their comfort zone. To start, you can try to put yourself in a position to take small risks. If a person has social anxiety, they could try to get a job in a coffee shop or somewhere where they will have to interact with a lot of people but on a limited level. This will get you thinking about how you can interact with people, and it will start to get you more comfortable with exposure to people every day. The more people that you interact with, the more you will start to learn that you are a cool and interesting person if you engage in good faith, and confidence will grow from there.

Confidence

Confidence is what lets you do what you should do—that little feeling that tells you should offer this person a job, or walk out of another situation, or drive a different route home—you do it because you are confident in yourself, and you have seen yourself succeed over and over. This is something that will need to take a little time, and you need to be patient and kind to yourself through this experience. There is no way to record intuition; there is no way to quantify it. This is something in your soul. It is something that might take some soul-searching to do. This is something that some people feel that come from your ancestors, and there is a sort of collective unison that we are all participating in together. The idea of the collective unconscious is that we are all human beings and can relate to each other one human level. This means that our intuition will often match.

Chapter 6: Understand Personality Types to Influence

There are many personality systems that have been redeveloped in the history of human study. Throughout time, people have engaged in self-reflexive exercises to explore what it means to be a human and why we are the way we are. One of these folks who studied what it meant to be a man was Carl Jung. Jung did a lot of writing and research on archetypes. Archetypes are relatable things that we all see in life. See, Jung thought that since we all had common experiences—the sun, the moon, the dark of night, and the light of day—these connect us with a collective unconscious. Humans have universal experiences—like birth and death, and love and heartbreak—and these universal themes suggest a psychic, pre-ordained order in our minds. This is the idea that since we are all in human bodies experiencing the earth, there must be a commonality in our experience. These archetypes might manifest themselves in different ways in different cultures, but they are deeply held within us.

Since we are all connected to our physical experience and the earth in a very intimate way, there are forms of ways of living and personality that have come out into the consciousness as recognizable ways that people are the way that they are. The shadow is a symbol of the unconscious, and it is an analogy for a person's dark side, in the eyes of Jung. The shadow self does mirror Freud's id and is the animal side to our consciousness. It is what makes us fully human, and it is the place that we go when we are feeling animalistic in any direction, i.e., satisfying a need to have sex, eat, or protect oneself.

Enneagram and Its Nine Types

Jung's work has been processed over and over again and has influenced many spheres of thinking, including popular psychology and scientific psychology. The Enneagram system is a system of personality that may have ties to Jung's work, as many of the principles that he looked at are found there. The Enneagram has its roots in the Sufi tradition, and it was refined over the years by various thinkers. The Enneagram of personality loosely aligns with Jung's idea of personality, and it presents nine personalities as ways that we can recognize people behaving in the world.

The Enneagram is not a magic scroll that will tell the future and tell you just how a person will act in any given situation. Rather, it is a way that you can think about personality and a way for you categorize people into behavioral patterns and tell why they are the way they are and why they do the things that they do. It is not something that is crystal clear in every case. A person who you see one day might act a certain way because they are feeling a certain way, but then the next day they will act completely different. This does not discredit the Enneagram, for, in fact, the Enneagram is one the closest things to describe the indescribable. Like Jung's stereotypes, these personality types can be deeply tied to literature, movies, etc., and we tend to see them over and over and over in art and literature.

The Perfectionist

The first personality type in the Enneagram of personality is the Perfectionist. The Perfectionist is driven by a moral drive. They are good people, and this is because they grow up wanting to be good people. The Perfectionist will often have pathology relating to perfectionism. If a Perfectionist is driven in childhood always to be achieving and always trying to be the best, they can often grow up with habits that relate to perfectionism that will become problems later in life. The Perfectionist wants everything not only to be working in good condition, but they also want things to be moral. They see the world in good and bad, and they definitely want to be on the good side of things.

The Perfectionist will need to learn to calm down their perfectionist urges to reach self-realization. Self-realization is eating concept of a person being able to be fully themselves and reach the potential theta they have in several different domains. These domains include but are not limited to leave, work, relationships, art, and whatever else a person needs to function. When a Perfectionist is able to realize that not everything needs to be perfect and that they can just reaccept what is going on around them, then they will be able to make more connections with other people and with themselves, and they will find that they have an easier time in life.

The Helper

The second personality in the Enneagram is the Helper. The Helper wants to help people out, and they want the world to be a better place. The Helper will often find a helping profession, where they are working with another bole to help them in their lives. They height have jobs like doctors, therapists, nurses, physical therapists, etc. These people have a deep drive to help and be helpful. They want to give and be generous with themselves, and they expect other people to do the same. The Helper often gets into codependent relationships, where they want to help another persona nod; they need the other person to need them. This can become an unhealthy dynamic, as the Helper is always looking for their next person to help even though the person will likely never change.

The helper must transition from this pattern if they want to engage in the practice that will lead to self-realization. A helper must realize that others can be helped, and they fill this role very well, but they must also acknowledge that they themselves need help nod; they must learn to help them and accept help from others. When the Helper does this, they will learn that the world is not a bad and scary place and that they can actually be in the world and be helped by others, and that this will provide them with a sense of contentment. It is all about balancing your key traits with the rest of your consciousness.

The Achiever

The third personality type in the Enneagram is the Achiever. The Achiever is a very optimistic and charismatic person. They like to go to the top of a mountain because they felt like it. Or, they might have seen someone else go partway up the mountain, and they want to prove that they can achieve something greater than someone else around them. Achieving provides a way for this person to find personal growth and feel good about them. The achiever will eventually realize that achieving is only one dimension of human life. Achieving is something that we do when we need to move society forward, and it is essential that we have achieved in the world. However, the Achiever will have to learn about other aspects of human life, including loving, resting, taking care of others, and reflection.

Once an Achiever is able to do this, they will learn that achievement is not needed for them to win the love of tether's they can have love just the way they are. Acceptance is going to Abe a big task for the Achiever as they go on in life and try to make deep connections with other people.

The Romantic

The next personality described in the Enneagram is the Romantic. The Romantic is driven by a deep need to make life meaningful, and they do it well. The Romantic loves oceans, fires, parties, sunsets, storytelling, drinks, coffee shops, bookstores, and the like. They want to live in one beautify moment forever. They want everything to be beautiful, and they enjoy the melancholy of life. They like to revel in the sadness fought life is, and they think of the human condition as a beautiful thing. The world rather is out on the road performing with a band than working in an office. They like to get lost in books and poetry, and they are usually good at conversations with others. The Romantic is oftentimes an artist, and they will often try to live as a musician, artist, actor, or radio host. They are people who are creative and spontaneous. One dark side of the Romantic is that they are prone to depression. This is because they feel so much in the world, and they are escapists because the world overwhelms them. They may not be very good at modulating their emptiness, not getting out of a certain mood state. They might feel that the world is too sad and dangerous for them, and this will often keep them in a depression.

In order to find self-realization, a Romantic will have to learn that not every moment in every day is beautiful. This will be where they need to find acceptance: not every day is beautiful, not every moment is a good moment. There are dry, humdrum moments that take up the better part of each day, and they will need to learn to cope with that. The Romantic will often be able to temper their earlier instincts for chaos and rebellion and find peace. They do this thought, acknowledging that the world is not always beautiful, but she is nothing they can do about that.

The Investigator

The next personality type on the Enneagram is the Investigator. The Investigator is driven by a need to perceive the world. They may web writers or journalists or scientists. They like to organize themselves in the world's sponge, somebody who is always receiving information from the world. They believe that by observing and investigating, they will find truth and meaning. They are driven by the need to perceive. The need to perceive is something that we all have within us, but the Investigator is obsessed with it. They might suffer from a lack of personality in the self because they're a lays focus used on tethers and other systems and bodies to be convened with, then to investigate them. In order to achieve self-realization, the investigator will need to learn how to turn that investigating light upon themselves and have space for self-reflection. The Instigator could be aligned with many different worldviews, but this doesn't change their core need to balance their urges. This will take the Investigator to have some sort of life-altering experience where they feel humbled. Only then will they be able to shine a light on the closet in their mind and really learn what is up with them.

The Loyalist

The next category of personality in the Enneagram is the Loyalist. The Loyalist wants to mother more in the world than friends. They don't like the physical intimacy of intimate relationships at first, and they are not so convened with family bonds. What they want are friends to surround them at all times and for them to have a full social circle with lots of different types of friends. The loyalist will often have a group, or they might just have a really good friend that they have found a symbiotic relationship with. They will find a person that they are able to accompany in the world and be loyal to, and the person who they are with will find ways to be a person that the person can be lay to. The Loyalist really dislikes conflict, and they will stave to avoid conflict at all costs. The Loyalist tends to get into a codependent relationship. Oftentimes, the Helper and the Loyalist will get into a codependent relationship weir the Helper wants to help the Loyal sis change, but the loyalist is not interested in changing, rather in prolonging the relationship. They will find themselves giving a little of what their other wanes at different times, and they will find that they get locked into relationships that are unhealthy and are really bad for them.

What the Loyalist needs to develop to reach self-realization is a sense of self and identity. They're so focused on themselves in the context of tethers, Althea the Loyalist will need to learn how to say what they want to see when they want to say it, and they will have to learn to be themselves around other people. Oftentimes, a loyalist will feel like the world has cheated them, that they were a good person and friend at theta they were not given in the same opportunity back to prove that they are the best. They will feel downtrodden and disappointed in the world, and they will need to take this feeling and learn to modulate it so that they are not feeling like they're the only person in the world who is feeling that way. The Loyalist often feels that the world has some crazy order to it that they can't figure out. The Loyalist will need to learn that that is not the case; actually, the world is similarly indeterminable to all people.

The Optimist

The Optimist is the social butterfly. This is a personality type from the Enneagram that loves to be with other people and loves to lift other people up. They are able to see the good in every situation, and they have fantastical drams about what old be in the future. The Optimist will be able to imagine realities that are not accessible to the everyday thinker, and they will vet driven by the need to fix, to achieve, and to bring people together. The optimist may be less of an achiever hand other, but hey have achievements in certain areas. The optimist loves to be able to light up a room and make people laugh, and they want to see everyone around them grow to their full potential. The optimist loves eating new people, and they love being around children. They think that life should be carefree and easy; they want everything to be a good time, and they want everyone to be partying all the time.

In order to reach self-actualization, the optimist will have to realize that the worlds are a somewhat pessimistic place, and they will have to get more in touch with their feelings of sadness and fief. This happens slowly unless omen kind of dramatic even happens to cause an ego death in the person. The next personality in the Enneagram system is the Protector. The Protector learned early on that this is a way they can control their environment: their own, sometimes physical, forces. They are good at helping other people out, but not in the same way as the Helper. They like to use butter strength to defeat their enemies and accomplish their goals. They are really good at sports, often, and they tend to be people who emphasize the physical form more than others. They see the physical form as a metaphor for the mind, and where the mind goes, the body will follow. They see themselves as having a role in the universe to tend to and take care of, to in an emotional sense, but more in the sense of watching out over a flock.

The Protector

The Protector will need to realize a few things in order to reach their potential as human beading. They will need to learn that they, like everyone else, have weaknesses, even physical ones, and they will learn to live with these deficiencies by earning to depend on other people. This will be hard for the Protector, as they really dislike exposing themselves to others, and they hate being vulnerable. The Protector is a person who will need to learn to embrace the inner child, and rather than telling them that they need to fight to survive, they will need to tell the inner child that it okay to cry, it is okay to be weak, it is okay to depend on others.

The Peacemaker

The final personality type that is presented by the Enneagram of personality is the Peacemaker. The Peacemaker is interested in harmony, and they like to be connected with other people whom they like to see to thrive in the community. The Peacemaker is driven by a moral compass, but not in a pathological way like the Perfectionist. Where the Perfectionism wants everything to be perfect because it is good, the Peacemaker was everything to be good because pall will experience less suffering that way. There is always a pain, but the Peacemaker knows that there are pain and offers. One of them, pain, is never going to leave our lives. There will be aspects of pain, whether it is physical or emotional, throughout our lives. It is not something that we can escape. Suffering, however, is something that happens when he tries to deal with pain and can't really dale with it all the way. Then, we are suffering. Ties are a state where we are fighting against being human, and it is the opposite of acceptance. The Peacemaker intuitively knows this situation, and they understand the dynamics of throw this works. They want to make the world a better place.

In order to make peace with the world for them, the Peacemaker must actually go the other way and learn how to be more of a fighter. This is the mistake that this personality type often faces: they don't realize that to enact the change that they would like to see in the world, they have to go out and do it. They may seem like meek or weak people, and they like to keep themselves out of battles. They need to be more like the Protector if they want to establish higher-level orders of consciousness. The Peacemaker knows when they are doing this. They must be able to learn how to stand up for themselves as well as others and to be assertive and fight the good fight.

More About the Enneagram

The way that these personality types are situated in the Enneagram has significance, too. There are triads and wings in the Enneagram system. These can be studied more if you are interested in the subject. The personality types presented here and other systems of personality basically give us a way to look at people and analyze their behavior. They can show us the way that people act in certain stations. They tell us about the innate drives of a person rather than just the venerable characteristics. You must be careful in trying to apply the knowledge of personality types to your everyday life and know that people might be tricky and may not be too easily figured out. On one day of the week, a person may be acting like a certain personality, and on another day, they might be acting like they are in a big mood that differs from the other day. Depending on whoever they want to be at the moment, something different is to be expected. However, there are certain ways that we orient ourselves in the world, and these contribute to our behavior. The personality types can tell you how to observe these and what to look for. There are many other systems of personality, which can open your perspective even more.

Personality is something that is not set in stone, but it does tend to be a way that a person functions and is not tantamount to the entire world, for most of their time. People can shift, however, and change in their lives. A person may have to actually make the shift from fitting in with one personality to an entire another personality type in their lifetime. It is not common, but it does happen. There are ways that you can derive some meaning from the personality types listed in the Enneagram, and they can be a good way for you to read people.

By being able to identify a perfectionist, for instance, you can then know why a person does what they do. When you realize that they might fit in well with the perfectionist personality type, then you can start to know that they want everything to be good and moral, and that is their highest motivation in life. Then, you can adjust your expectations accordingly.

A big part of what the Enneagram allows for is for youth are able to adjust your expectations of a person. Lots of people think about everyone as having the same characteristics as them. Some people may have similar patterns and characteristics as you, but many do not. Expectations allow for you to be able to know what a person will be vale to handle, what a person will bearable to do in certain situations, and how much you can depend on them.

There are different thresholds that we all have in different areas. One of them is the discomfort threshold. Many people have high discomfort thresholds, and they are able to withstand certain types of pain better and longer than others. Some people have high emotional pain tolerances and low physical pain tolerances. Other people will have the opposite experience: physical pain will be easy for them to endure, but the emotional pain of vulnerability will be difficult.

The teachings of G.I. Gurdjieff and Oscar Ichazo have much to do with the Enneagram gaining as much prominence as it has in recent decades. Ichazo and Gurdjieff were teaching far away from each other, using different methods and languages, but their common interest of helping people to become their deepest authentic selves through a program of inner work. Gurdjieff worked and lived in Russia and then France. Ichazo established a school in Chile in the 1960s, where he taught his way of using the Enneagram for self-analysis.

Gurdjieff was the one who connected a Platonic-inflected conception of essence versus form in his teachings. He taught that one had both an essence and a personality. The essence of a person is their nature; it is some inherent truth of their being. It is the nature of a person. The personality is what has arisen from the context and circumstances that we grow up and develop with. The way to finding one's essential self, to Gurdjieff, was spending time in a rigorous program of observing oneself, and that we all individually and collectively need to strive for transformation to evolve.

Now, an important part of considering the Enneagram and unlocking these personality types to understand others better and improve communication is that each person is a microcosm of the whole system. That is to say that all nine types think, feel, have a sex drive, a drive for self-perseveration, and social impulses. All nine types have strengths and faults. So, in parsing your own type and other personality types, you must remain conscious of the common attitudes that we have, and also the contextual factors for personality. Betty, in the office, may only be showing you one side of her that will lead you to think she's a Protector. But in most of her life, she is the Loyalist. When she is challenged to an extreme, she behaves like The Investigator. We may embody many different aspects of each of the personalities, but if you were able to look closer into Betty's life, you'd see that she has core attitudes and developmental tendencies that align with the drives of one type. Oscar Ichazo is largely responsible for the Enneagram system of personality that most people work with today. Ichazo initially labeled the system of self-analysis used to work with the Enneagram as "protoanalysis." He had one particularly bright student named Claudio Naranjo. Naranjo studied with Ichazo, and he carried over Ichazo's teachings to California in the early '70s. Naranjo led groups of people participating in protoanalysis and taught about the personality types. Naranjo was born in Chile but had trained in the United States as a psychiatrist. He took many different perspectives into consideration in his development and teachings, including Jungian archetypes, the work of Karen Horney, existential philosophy, psychoanalysis, and the work of G.I. Gurdjieff. The Enneagram struck him as a powerful tool for personal growth and an integrative model of personality.

The teachings of Gurdjieff, Ichazo, and Naranjo fall into several different categories of study. Some have suggested the term "psycho-spiritual," that is, addressing problems of both psychology and spirituality. When we compare the psycho-spiritual system of teachings presented by Gurdjieff, Ichazo, and Naranjo to psychoanalysis, we see a great number of similarities. Both theories of the Enneagram and psychoanalytic theory view personality as a result of the interaction of a child with the world. They both want to take into account the child's innate disposition and the child's environment. One difference is that psychoanalytic theory focuses a little more on childhood, and the Enneagram is applicable equally to children and adults.

There is a holistic quality to the Enneagram system of personality. It directs our attention to the tripartite division that we all experience in the head, the heart, and the body. This is mirrored in the intellect, emotion, and behavior. The Enneagram supports an equal consideration of body and mind, as often seen to non-western philosophy. The Enneagram supports a balance of these three for functioning.

Conclusion

Thank you for making it through to the end of *Influence Human Behavior*! Let's hope it was informative and able to provide you with all of the tools you need to achieve your goals—whatever they may be.

The next step is to try and apply these concepts in your daily life. Good luck!

Finally, if you found this book useful in any way, a review on Amazon is always appreciated!

Description

Influence and persuasion are a huge part of our everyday lives—from large-scale persuasion, like ad campaigns and political messaging, to small-scale influence, like the car salesman trying to get a few more bucks out of you. There exists persuasion in all aspects of life. Trying to sort through all the persuasion and influence can leave people feeling confused, disoriented, and wondering how to act.

This book is all about centering yourself, learning to speak for yourself, and learning to differentiate all the voices that always seem to be aimed at you. In order to be a persuasive person, you have to have your ducks in a row. Psychologically speaking, this means that you must have a realistic and positive view of yourself. There are many people in the world who have unfinished business and baggage that they carry around with them. The point of this book is to help you let go of that baggage and finish your business. What might this unfinished business be? Whatever it is, it might be affecting your level of anxiety. This must be addressed because those who are always caught up in their own emotional states will be more susceptible to persuasion. A person who can defend themselves from persuasion is a person who feels confident, can speak up when they need to, and has the experience of standing up for themselves.

The power of fear keeps many people down. Fear of failure (or even success), social interaction, rejection, and difficulty—these are the fears that most of us experience on a daily basis. Fear is a part of life, and fear is powerful. In fact, a lot of persuasions are based on fear and appeals to the fears that we keep with us in our lives. Fear can keep us quiet at home. It can keep us away from what we love. You need to be able to face your fears to become the person who you need to be.

Part of this is being able to read people and know personality types. In this book, a bit of information about personality types is presented so that you can have an idea of the basic ways that people tend to be. Reading people is important in the defense against persuasion because if you can read someone, you can tell what they want from you.

Building empathy for yourself and others is key. Empathy is the ability to feel with other people, and it is different from sympathy. Sympathy is when you are able to understand someone else's situation and feel for them. Empathy, on the other hand, is being able to understand someone's situation and feel *with* them. This means that you are able to share their experiences and truly be with them. This book covers how to develop this skill, as well as:

Finding out what people really want

Reading people

Making others feel comfortable around you

Psychology basics

How to apply psychology

Emotions

Anxiety

How we become susceptible to persuasion

The power of fears

Relationship between neutrality and thinking

Personality types

Influence

Positive psychology

Tools for self-esteem

And much more!

Printed in Great Britain
by Amazon

40809303R00071